1250

5/80

S0-BCN-238

BULLETIN

COPY

Perspectives in American History

No. 55
THE RISE OF THE MISSIONARY SPIRIT
IN AMERICA 1790-1815

THE RISE OF THE MISSIONARY SPIRIT IN AMERICA

1790-1815

BY

OLIVER WENDELL ELSBREE, A.M.

Associate Professor of History, Bucknell University

PORCUPINE PRESS

Philadelphia

First edition 1928
(Williamsport: The Williamsport Printing and
Binding Co., 1928)

Reprinted 1980 by
PORCUPINE PRESS INC.
Philadelphia, PA 19107

BV
2410
.E67
1980

Library of Congress Cataloging in Publication Data

Elsbree, Oliver Wendell, 1889-
  The rise of the missionary spirit in America, 1790-1815.

  (Perspectives in American history ; no. 55)
  Reprint of the author's thesis, Columbia University, 1928.
  Vita.
  Bibliography: p.
  Includes index.
  1.   Missions,   American — History.   2.   Missions
— United   States — History.   I.   Title.   II.   Series:
Perspectives in American history (Philadelphia) ; no. 55.
BV2410.E6   266   79-13028
ISBN 0-87991-376-2

Manufactured in the United States of America

PREFACE

It is no longer necessary for the student of American history to apologize for departing from the field of "politics" in selecting a subject for special investigation. Economic and social factors are readily conceded their proper niche in the historical edifice. Too little stress, it would seem, however, has been placed on religious ideas and practices as factors in the complex social structure of those whose words and acts constitute the raw materials of history. Until quite recent times most writers of books dealing with American history have been content to relegate the religious phase to the Church historians. The tacit assumption that religion is something compartmentally separate from political and social phenomena grows in part from the traditional theory of the complete separation of Church and State in the United States. Although the impact of a better social psychology is slowly changing this attitude, at the present moment it is safe to say that few indeed have been the efforts to weave together the religious with the other strands, and to make something of a synthesis of American society in its varied interrelations.

Nor have many American Church historians succeeded in linking religious life and thought as significant modes of human behavior with other attitudes and beliefs of social groups within a given period. Most of them have been content to merely chronicle the developments of the numerous Protestant denominations which have flourished on American soil. So frankly apologetic are many of these denominational histories that their value as interpretations of the past is slight. And in those rare instances where the denominational chronicles are critical and balanced they are likely to lack perspective. The readers of one denominational history usually learn little about other religious groups, even of denominations structurally and doctrin-

3

ally similar. The chief value of denominational histories is that they furnish the investigator material for his synthesis. Beyond that they have thus far achieved little.

It was with the purpose of determining just what might be done in the way of a social study of American religious ideas as they were being slowly but effectively changed by missionary appeals during the quarter century before 1815 that the writer of this treatise began over two years ago to gather his data. Such a study would have been impossible without the generous co-operation of many librarians whose personal interest in the work of the writer will be remembered with gratitude. The valuable collections of source and secondary materials to be found in the Libraries of Columbia University, the New York Historical Society, Union Theological Seminary, the Maine Historical Society, and Crozer Theological Seminary, the New York and Boston Public Libraries, and the University and Day Missions Libraries of Yale University were freely placed at his disposal. The writer feels particularly indebted to Professor Evarts B. Greene and Professor William R. Shepherd of Columbia University and to Dr. William W. Rockwell of Union Theological Seminary for valuable criticisms and suggestions and for aid in completing the bibliography. He desires to make due acknowledgment, however inadequate it must necessarily be, to Professor Harry R. Warfel of Bucknell University, who has offered invaluable advice and who sacrificed many hours in reading the proof. And finally, to Professor Dixon R. Fox of Columbia University, under whose direction this study was planned and whose interest in it throughout has been to its author a source of inspiration, is to be attributed much of the merit the finished product may chance to have. For all shortcomings and imperfections the writer alone is responsible.

Lewisburg, Pa.
    March 1, 1928.

CONTENTS

5

CHAPTER I

PIONEER PROTESTANT MISSIONARIES AMONG THE AMERICAN INDIANS DURING THE SEVENTEENTH AND EIGHTEENTH CENTURIES

In each of three ill-starred attempts of Englishmen to found colonies during the last quarter of the sixteenth century there was involved a plan for the propagation of the gospel among the natives of North America. The unity of Church and State in Elizabethan England made the extension of ecclesiastical control corollary to the establishment of civil jurisdiction over newly occupied regions. Such extensions of religious authority would seem to be but indirectly related to missionary enterprises, yet they furnish the background for a study of the origin of American missions. The first of these efforts to attach the American natives to the Anglican Church was that made by Chaplain Wolfall who accompanied Martin Frobisher on his third voyage overseas and whose task it was not only to serve his white constituency but also "to reform these infidels [the natives] to Christianitie." (1) Likewise, Sir Humphrey Gilbert, when he obtained his patent for discovery, was invested with authority to establish in his colonies "the true Christian faith or religion now professed in the Church of England." (2) Both Frobisher and Gilbert failed to establish permanent colonies, and no results attended the efforts of their clergy to convert the savages.

The name "Virginia" has survived to remind us of Sir Walter Raleigh and his premature hopes. Among his Roanoke

---

(1) William S. Perry. *The History of the American Episcopal Church,* 1587-1883, vol. i, p. 7.
(2) *Ibid.,* p. 9.

7

colonists was Thomas Hariot who preached Christianity to the natives. A native "Lord" whose name was Manteo was baptized in 1587—probably the first red man to be received into a Protestant church in America. Raleigh showed his special interest in the religious welfare of the natives by donating £100 to the Virginia Company "for the propagation of the Christian religion in Virginia." (3) His colony, however, was completely wiped out in some unknown manner. The relief expedition which went out in search of it in 1590 found not a trace of it.

The first charter of the Virginia Company, which in 1607 founded Jamestown, showed concern for the aborigines and commended the missionary motive. Article III of the charter read: "We greatly commending, and graciously accepting of, their desire for the Furtherance of so noble a Work, which may, by the Providence of Almighty God, hereafter tend to the Glory of his Divine Majesty, in propagating the Christian Religion to such people as yet live in Darkness and Miserable Ignorance of the true Knowledge and Worship of God, and may in time bring the Infidels and Savages, living in these parts to human civility, and to a settled and quiet Government: do by these our Letters Patents, graciously accept of, and agree to, their humble and well intended desires." (4)

The most noted of the early Virginia missionaries was Alexander Whitaker who was afterward known as "the Apostle to the Indians." Among the native children whom he undertook to civilize and Christianize was the famous maiden Pocahontas. For over a decade the missionary labors of Whitaker and his aides seemed to be making satisfactory progress, but in 1622 there occurred one of the worst Indian massacres in the history of the colony, which brought Whitaker's work to an abrupt end. No further efforts were made to evangelize the Indians of Virginia until late in the seventeenth century when William and Mary College was established for the education of the youth of

(3)   Ibid., pp. 18, 19.
(4)   William Stith, The History of the First Discovery and Settlement of Virginia. Appendix I, pp. 1, 2.

white colonists and of Indians. Indian education, however, proved to be of slight importance in the history of William and Mary. (5)

In New England the Pilgrims and the Puritans who settled in eastern Massachusetts together with those dissenters who soon afterward founded Connecticut and Rhode Island were interested in the spiritual welfare of the red men. Governor Bradford of Plymouth, in his enumeration of reasons why the Pilgrims wished to leave the Netherlands, said: "Lastly, (and which was not least) a great hope, and inward zeal they had of laying some good foundation, (or at least to make some way thereunto) for the propagating, and advancing the Gospel of the kingdom of Christ in those remote parts of the world; yea, though they should be but even as stepping stones unto others for the performing of so great a work." (6) The weakness of the colony, however, rendered impossible any concerted missionary efforts on the part of the first settlers. Roger Williams seems to have preached to the Indians while living at Plymouth, for he said in his *Key to the Language of America* that "God was pleased to give me a painful, patient spirit to lodge with them in their filthy smoky holes, (even while I lived at Plymouth and Salem) to gain their tongues," and that he had preached to them "many hundreds of times, to their great delight and great convictions." (7) Later in the century the pastor of the Plymouth church, John Cotton, (8) was regularly preaching to five congregations of Indians in his vicinity, and Samuel Treat and Richard Bourn were attempting to civilize and Christianize six congregations of natives living on Cape Cod. (9) None of these missions, however, was destined

---

(5) W. S. Perry, *op. cit.*, vol. i, chap. 5. "The University of Henrico and efforts for the conversion of the savages."

(6) William Bradford, *History of Plymouth Plantation*, vol. i, p. 55.

(7) Roger Williams, *A Key into the Language of America*, pp. 3-5.

(8) Not to be confused with John Cotton of Boston.

(9) David McClure, *Memoirs of the Rev. Eleazar Wheelock*, pp. 93, 94; Herbert L. Osgood, *The American Colonies in the Seventeenth Century*, vol. i, p. 539.

to acquire the fame of that established by John Eliot, near Boston.

Among the powers granted by charter to the officials of the Massachusetts Bay Company which settled in Boston and its vicinity, there was included "the directing, ruling, and disposeing of all other matters and thinges whereby our said people, inhabitants there, maie be soe religiously, peaceablie, and civilly governed, as their good life and orderlie conversacon maie wynn and incite the natives of country to the knowledg and obedience of the onlie true God and Savior of mankinde, and the Christian fayth, which, in our royall intencon and the adventurers free profession, is the principall ende of this plantacon." (10) It was therefore in accordance with this "principall ende" that John Eliot, who came to Boston in 1631 in consequence of the persecutions of Archbishop Laud, began his study of the Mohican language with a view to the evangelization of the Indians of eastern Massachusetts. He began preaching to them in 1646, and fifteen years later published the first part of his famous Mohican Bible. Like many another early missionary among the Indians, Eliot suspected that they might be the Ten Lost Tribes of Israel. If so, their conversion to Christianity would prove of more than ordinary importance for the Kingdom of God in that it would fulfill prophecy. For nearly fifty years he strove to raise the standards of living among the former inhabitants of the forest. His method was to organize villages of Indians who were thereafter governed in accordance with the Mosaic code. A common house served in each village as school and

---

(10)   *Records of the Governor and Company of the Massachusetts Bay in New England,* vol. i, p. 17.

Similar phraseology was adopted by Charles II in the charter granted to Connecticut in 1662. The part relating to the promotion of religion reads: "and for the directing, ruleing and disposeing of all other matters and things whereby our said people, Inhabitants there, may bee soe religiously, peaceably, and civilly governed as their good life and orderly conversacon may wynn and invite the natives of the country to the knowledge and obedience of the onely true God and Saviour of mankind, and the Christian faith, which in our Royall intencons and the adventurers free profession is the onely and principall ende of this Plantacon." (*Public Records of Connecticut,* vol. ii, p. 8.)

church. In the schools, both children and adults were regularly catechized in the faith. Husbandry and the mechanic arts were taught in the hope that the Indians would permanently abandon their savage ways of living. In all, fourteen towns were established, but eight of them were completely destroyed during King Philip's War, and the others gradually disappeared after Eliot's death in 1690. Like Whitaker of Virginia, Eliot was known by later generations as "the Apostle to the Indians." (11)

Eliot's efforts to Christianize the American aborigines attracted attention in England and led to the organization of the first Protestant missionary society in the British Isles. An act passed by the Long Parliament in 1649 (the memorable year in which Charles I was executed) created "the President and Society for propagation of the Gospel in New England." (12) Collections for its support were taken in Cromwell's army, as well as in the churches, and £12,000 was realized. This society gave £50 annually to the support of its American agents, among whom were to be numbered John Eliot, two of the Mayhews, John Sergeant, and Jonathan Edwards. (13) After the restoration of Charles II, the society was reorganized under the presidency of Sir Robert Boyle, a noted physicist and chemist, who directed its activities for the next three decades. Boyle was also prominent in helping to found another philanthropic organization, the Christian Faith Society, which aimed at the conversion and education of negro slaves in the British West Indies. After Boyle's death the Christian Faith Society sought to carry out a plan for the conversion of the Indians through the establish-

(11)   *New York Missionary Magazine,* 1801, pp. 162-166. *The Adviser or Vermont Evangelical Magazine,* August, 1809. Articles in *The Connecticut Evangelical Magazine* from Feb., 1802 to March, 1809, entitled, "Attempts to Christianize the Indians in New England."

(12)   C. H. Firth and R. S. Rait (editors), *Acts and ordinances of the interregnum,* 1642-1660, vol. ii, pp. 197-200. Act for the promoting and propagating the Gospel of Jesus Christ in New England, July 27, 1649.

(13)   H. L. Osgood, *op. cit.,* vol. i, pp. 422, 423. A. C. Thompson, *Protestant Missions,* p. 52; Wardlaw Thompson and Arthur M. Johnson, *British Foreign Missions,* p. 2.

ment of William and Mary College in Virginia, (14) but as has been noted above, Indian education did not prosper there.

Unique in the annals of missionary endeavors among the red men were the continuous services rendered the so-called Island Indians by no less than five generations of a famous family named Mayhew. In 1642 the elder Thomas Mayhew secured a grant of Martha's Vineyard, and some neighboring islands and, much after the fashion of an English lord, was impelled to attend to the spiritual welfare of his subjects. Accordingly he settled his son Thomas as pastor over the English inhabitants and as missionary to the Indians of the Vineyard. About one hundred of the natives had accepted Christianity when the younger Thomas Mayhew lost his life at sea in 1652, and during the next twenty-four years the father, although an old man, continued the work. Before the death of the latter, three-fourths of all the natives of Martha's Vineyard were listed as "praying Indians." John Mayhew, grandson of the founder of the colony, next took up the work of the Indian mission, and from him the leadership passed on down the Mayhew line, first to his son Experience who spoke the language of the natives from childhood, and then to Zechariah, son of Experience, who died in 1806 at the age of eighty-nine, having spent the greater part of his life in the service of the red men. (15)

The efforts of Eliot and the first Mayhews to civilize the Indians of Massachusetts were reinforced by the cooperation of the promoters of the only New England college established dur-

(14)   Charles H. Robinson, *History of Christian Missions*, p. 57.

(15)   W. A. Hallock, *The Venerable Mayhews and the Aboriginal Indians of Martha's Vineyard*, passim. Cotton Mather, *Magnalia Christi Americana*, vol. i, p. 568. See also, *Some correspondence between the Governors and Treasurers of the New England Company in London and the Commissioners of the United Colonies in America, the missionaries of the Company and others, between the years 1657 and 1712, to which are added the Journals of the Rev. Experience Mayhew in 1713 and 1714.* (Proceedings of the Massechusetts Historical Society, June, 1920).

ing the seventeenth century. The charter of Harvard College, secured in 1650, listed among the designs of the institution, "the education of English and Indian youth of the country in knowledge and godliness." (16) The Society for Propagating the Gospel in New England provided funds for the erection of an Indian college, but the plan proved impracticable. A fund, however, was raised by private subscription for the purpose of instructing the natives. It was this fund that Edward Randolph sought to divert to the support of the Anglican clergy in New England, on the ground that it was not being applied to its original purpose. (17) Randolph, however, failed to carry through his scheme, and the fund remained to be used in financing missionaries among the Marshpee Indians on Cape Cod and the Vineyard Indians under Zechariah Mayhew. (18)

Among early Protestant missionary enterprises among the Indians are to be noted the labors of Johannes Megapolensis who came to New Netherland from Holland in 1642 and in the following year began preaching to the Mohawk Indians near Albany, then called Fort Orange. Megapolensis is not to be regarded as the first Protestant missionary to the red men of America as some have insisted, because Roger Williams certainly preached tō the Indians of Salem and Plymouth before 1635, but his work antedated that of Eliot by three years and doubtless was of more permanent value than the unorganized and unsystematic evangelism of Williams. Megapolensis became proficient in the Mohawk language and baptized quite a number of the natives. (19) After 1649 he was pastor of the Reformed congregation at New

---

(16)   Josiah Quincy, *History of Harvard College*, vol. i, p. 46.

(17)   *Ibid.*, vol. i, pp. 192, 353-355; H. L. Osgood, *op. cit.*, vol. iii, p. 391.

(18)   Jedidiah Morse, Sermon, Nov. 1, 1810, before the Society for Propagating the Gospel among the Indians and Others in North America.

(19)   Charles E. Corwin, *A Manual of the Reformed Church in America*, 1628-1922, p. 180.

Amsterdam and had little opportunity to engage in missionary efforts. (20)

The Revolution of 1688 in England, terminating as it did in the victory of the Established Church and the parliamentary party over the Catholic King, James II, made possible the launching of new projects for the extension of ecclesiastical control over dissenters in the colonies and "for the encouragement of the Christian Education of our Negro and Indian children." (21) Foremost among the promoters of colonial missions was Dr. Thomas Bray of Warwickshire who was made ecclesiastical commissary for Maryland in 1696. Three societies of a missionary character were formed in response to Bray's earnest appeals, namely, the Society for Promoting Christian Knowledge (1698), the Society for the Propagation of the Gospel in Foreign Parts (1701), and an organization known as "the Associates of Dr. Bray" (1723) (22). Of these organizations the Society for the Propagation of the Gospel in Foreign Parts, or the S. P. G. as it was sometimes called, was the most significant missionary agency of the Anglican Church in the American colonies. (23)

(20)   A letter from the Dutch ministers, Megapolensis and Drisius, to the classis of Amsterdam, dated August 5, 1657, discloses the fact that the Indians encountered by the Reformed missionaries differed in no respect from the savages the Puritans were attempting to civilize, in their tendency to backslide from the civilized manners they were supposed to have adopted. The letter said: "We have had an Indian here with us for about two years. He can read and write Dutch very well. We have instructed him in the fundamental principles of our religion, and he answers publicly in church, and can repeat the Commandments. We have given him a Bible, hoping he might do some good among the Indians, but it all resulted in nothing. He took to drinking brandy, he pawned the Bible, and turned into a regular beast, doing more harm than good among the Indians." *Original Narratives of Early American History*, vol. viii, p. 399.

(21)   W. S. Perry (editor), *Papers relating to the history of the Church in Virginia*, 1650-1776, p. 112. Letter from James Blair, Ecclesiastical Commissary for Virginia to the Archbishop of Canterbury.

(22)   Marcus W. Jernegan, Slavery and Conversion in the American Colonies. *American Historical Review*, vol. xxi, pp. 509-511.

(23)   Evarts B. Greene, The Anglican Outlook on the American Colonies in the early eighteenth century. *American Historical Review*, vol. xx, pp. 64-85.

The first missionaries of the S. P. G. were George Keith and John Talbot who, under its direction, made a tour of observation from the Piscataqua river in New England to Caratuck in North Carolina. The real purpose of this journey seems clearly to have been the conversion of Quakers and other dissenters to Anglicanism, rather than the evangelization of the Indians. Little was accomplished by the itinerants and shortly afterward Keith returned to England, while Talbot settled as pastor at Burlington, New Jersey. (24)

The workers of the S. P. G. who succeeded Keith and Talbot were instructed to convert and educate the negro slaves in the colonies. (25) Opposition to the project was encountered in New England where the Puritan leaders were fearful lest the missionary enterprise of the Anglicans prove a lever for the establishment of the Episcopate in America. J. Usher, one of the missionaries stationed in Connecticut, wrote the Society, in 1730, that "sundry negroes" had made application for baptism, but that he was "not permitted to comply with their requests ...... being forbid by their masters." (26) Antagonism on the part of masters, however, to the Christianizing of slaves was by no means confined to New England, but was encountered in all the colonies where the S. P. G. missionaries labored. (27) The failure of all their efforts to Christianize the Chickasaw Indians in Georgia was likewise attributed to the shortcomings of the white settlers. Samuel Frink, a missionary of the S. P. G., writing in 1766 thus summarized the situation, accounting for his inability to produce any permanent effect upon the red men by saying that the white population of the region was as "destitute

(24) W. S. Perry, *History of the American Episcopal Church*, vol. i, chap. 12. For a discussion of the controversy which later arose over the supposed consecration of Talbot to the Episcopate see *ibid.*, vol. i, Monograph V, by John Fulton.

(25) *Classified Digest of the Records of the Society for the Propagation of the Gospel in Foreign Parts, 1701-1892*, pp. 837-845.

(26) *Ibid.*, p. 46.

(27) M. W. Jernegan, *op. cit.*, pp. 526-527.

of a sense of religion as the natives themselves." (28) Despite all discouragements, however, the S. P. G. was supporting seventy-seven workers in the American colonies when the Revolutionary war began. (29)

Notable among the designs for evangelizing the Indians of North America was that of the famous Bishop Berkeley of Cloyne. In 1725 Berkeley published "A Scheme for converting the Savage Americans to Christianity, by a college to be erected in the Summer Islands, otherwise called the Isles of Bermuda." Robert Walpole promised Berkeley £20,000 for the establishment of the college, but the opposition Berkeley encountered from other influential men in Great Britain led to the collapse of his dream. No effort was ever made to revive the "Scheme," although Berkeley had been in America advocating his idea for three years. (30)

Of much greater significance for the American Indian Missionary enterprise was the organization, in 1709, of the Society in Scotland for Propagating Christian Knowledge. It was customarily styled "The Scotch Society" to distinguish it from Bray's Anglican S. P. C. K. Its missionary work at the outset was con-

(28) *Digest of S. P. G. records,* p. 28.

(29) *Ibid., p.* 80. Some missionary work was undertaken by the S. P. G. among the Mohawk and Oneida Indians of New York through two Dutch Reformed ministers from Albany and Schenectady, Dellius and Freeman. John Ogilvie, a chaplain in the royal American regiment which made an expedition to Niagara in 1760, reported that Protestant missionaries had made little impression on the Iroquois, except that some of the Mohawks and Oneidas regularly attended Anglican services. (W. S. Perry, *Hist. Am. Epis. Ch.,* vol. i, p. 329). Earlier in the century (1712) the S. P. G. had sent one of its own workers to the Iroquois Indians, but the mission was abandoned after a few years. The desire of the English to secure the friendship of the Iroquois for political reasons seems evidently to have motivated the directors of the Society when they first gave consideration to the conversion of the red heathen in America. (C. F. Pascoe, *Two Hundred Years of the S. P. G.,* pp. 70, 71; E. B. Greene, The Anglican Outlook on the American Colonies, pp. 72, 73; *Classified Digest of S. P. G. Records, passim.*

(30) William Brown, *History of the Propagation of Christianity among the Heathen,* vol. iii, pp. 479, 480.

fined to the remote regions of Scotland, but, in 1730, a board of Correspondents was established in Boston with a view to the extension of missionary operations in America. The Boston Board was suspended in 1737, but four years later another was constituted in New York to direct Indian missions in New York, New Jersey, and Pennsylvania. In 1769 a Board made up of the Trustees of the College of New Jersey began to act in the capacity of Commissioners of the Scotch Society.

The New York Commissioners began their Indian missionary enterprise by employing Azariah Horton to work among the Indians on Long Island. Horton's mission, however, had to be abandoned after twelve years. (31) In the meantime David Brainerd had won fame as a pioneer missionary of the Scotch Society among the Indians of New Jersey. Brainerd's first labors were at Kaunameek, an Indian settlement midway between Albany, N. Y., and Stockbridge, Mass. There he remained for one year and established a school for the Indian children. Upon the advice of the Commissioners, however, the Indians were moved to Stockbridge, to be under the care of John Sergeant, while Brainerd was sent to the forks of the Delaware River in Pennsylvania near Easton. He made three visits to the Indians on the Susquehanna, 120 miles away, at gatherings of several tribes. He was more successful in his labors with the natives of Crossweeksung, New Jersey, whom he induced to move to a place near Cranbury, called Bethel, to receive regular religious instruction. At the age of twenty-nine, Brainerd died in Northampton, Mass., of pulmonary consumption. He had gone to New England seeking the help of a physician, but the privations he had undergone during the past five years had undermined his feeble body, and any relief he might have found was sought too late. (32)

An account of the Life of the late Reverend Mr. David

(31)   *Panoplist*, Aug., 1805, p. 117; W. D. Love, *Samson Occom*, pp. 12, 13.
(32)   Jonathan Edwards, *Life of David Brainerd, passim.*

Brainerd was published in Boston in 1749. Jonathan Edwards was its author, or rather editor, as the material was nearly all compiled from Brainerd's diary. This book had an influence which was altogether out of proportion to its value, owing to several factors which served to focus unusual attention upon it. In the first place, the youth of Brainerd and his attachment to Jerusha Edwards, who cared for him during his fatal illness, and who survived him by only four months, to be buried by his side in the cemetery at Northampton, made a powerful appeal to the popular imagination. Then, the compilation of his Journal by Edwards served to emphasize the place Brainerd had in the mind of this great theologian and divine. It is important to note that Brainerd, in his journal, reiterated on almost every page his own worthlessness and his utter despondency, the futility of all that he was trying to do, and the marvel that God would deign to even look with favor upon such a loathsome creature. How much of his melancholy and despondency, his morbid introspection, was due to the progress of disease, it is difficult to say. Certain it is that the life he lived, the pitiful story he told of suffering and privation, and the premature death he died, all served to focus the attention of at least two generations of people upon the heroism and devotion of youth to disinterested benevolence. Henry Martyn was influenced in deciding his life work by reading Brainerd's Diary. (33) William Carey likewise read the life of Brainerd and decided to become a missionary. (34) Fifty years after Brainerd's history was published, Bishop Asbury, of the Methodist Episcopal Church, wrote in his diary:

I reflected with pain, that we had never reprinted, in America, the life, labours, travels, and sufferings of that great man of God, David Brainerd of gracious memory; it would be a book well fitted for our poor, painful and faithful missionaries—none but God and themselves know what they suffer . . . . (35)

(33)   George Smith, *Henry Martyn, Saint and Scholar*, pp. 33, 60.
(34)   L. C. Barnes, *Two Thousand Years of Missions before Carey*, pp. 416, 417.
(35)   Francis Asbury, *Journal*, vol. ii, p. 310.

On the other hand, Lyman Beecher described the book as likely to produce a condition, "not spiritual but a state of permanent hypochondria." (36)

David Brainerd's work among the Indians of Cranbury was continued after his death by his brother John, a graduate of Yale College and a trustee of the College of New Jersey. John Brainerd spent the better part of his life in preaching to the poor whites of the New Jersey Pine country, and to the Indians of Cranbury and Brotherton, N. J. The Provincial government gave the Indians four thousand acres of land, but John Brainerd's missionary work was completely disrupted by the Revolutionary War. He died in 1781 at Deerfield, N. J., whither he had moved a few years before, leaving his few Indian wards in the care of Daniel Simon, an ordained Indian preacher. (37) Simon, however, revealed a typical Indian weakness for strong drink, and was suspended from the ministry. A considerable proportion of the feeble remnant of New Jersey Indians who remained after the War relapsed to paganism. In 1802 eighty-five Christians were all that were left as tangible evidence of the missionary labors of the Brainerds. They were removed to New Stockbridge, N. Y., where they were placed under the care of the younger John Sergeant. (38)

The elder John Sergeant was a contemporary of David Brainerd. He was employed by the New England Corporation to labor among the Indians whom he collected at Stockbridge, Mass. In 1734 he began his work at Housatonic among the so-called River Indians, who had been scattered throughout the region of northwestern Connecticut, western Massachusetts, and the adjacent counties in the province of New York. He learned the Indian tongue and sought to promote Christianity among the red men through a school which he set up at Stockbridge for the instruction of Indian youth who would go out as missionaries to

(36)   Lyman Beecher, *Autobiography*, vol. i, p. 47.
(37)   Thomas Brainerd, *Life of John Brainerd, passim.*
(38)   Miron Winslow, *A Sketch of Missions*, pp. 71-79.

their people. Opposition was encountered in the Dutch traders, who feared the effect of missions on commerce. Private benefactors, both in England and America, supplemented the meager salary allowed Mr. Sergeant by the New England Corporation. Isaac Hollis, Mr. and Mrs. Samuel Holden, Dr. Watts and others of London, and Governor Belcher and Dr. Benjamin Colman of Boston contributed to the support of Sergeant and his assistant. In 1745 the Prince of Wales was induced to head a subscription list for Sergeant's school. Like David Brainerd, Sergeant made a tour to the Indian settlements in Pennsylvania. He died prematurely in 1749. (39)

In 1743, the year David Brainerd began his Indian missionary labors, Eleazar Wheelock of Lebanon, Connecticut, received an Indian youth by the name of Samson Occom into a private school which he was conducting. As a result of Wheelock's experiment with Occom, an Indian mission school was established which was known after 1754 as Moor's Charity School. (40) There were about twenty young Indians attending the Charity School in 1762. (41) The institution was supported by private benefaction, by legislative appropriations made by Massachusetts and Connecticut, and by the Boston Board of Commissioners who represented the Scotch Society for Propagating Christian Knowledge. The Boston Board had been reconstituted in 1756. In 1763 it arranged with Samson Occom and David Fowler, both Indians, to go as missionaries to the Oneida Indians in Central New York. Three years later Occom and Nathaniel Whitaker went to Europe to solicit aid for the school. Occom's reception was most cordial. He was permitted to preach in England and Scotland where he succeeded in securing in all over £10,000 for his project. (42) The site of the school was changed in 1770 to Hanover, N. H., and it was managed under Wheelock's presidency in con-

(39)   *Panoplist,* Jan., Feb., and Mch., 1807; L. C. Barnes, *op. cit.*
(40)   Frederick Chase, *A History of Dartmouth College,* vol. i, pp. 7, 8.
(41)   *Ibid.,* pp. 2, 3,
(42)   *Ibid.,* p. 59.

nection with Dartmouth College, but the funds of the two institutions were separately administered. (43)

With the exception of Samson Occom, practically none of Wheelock's Indian pupils fulfilled his hopes. Joseph Brant was among those who, after accepting the training of the school, returned to a life of savage warfare. Occom remained loyal to his benefactors and spent the better part of his life in a seemingly futile effort to induce the Indians to refrain from deeds of savagery and to accept the civilized ways of the whites. During the Revolution all the Iroquois tribes were hostile to the missionaries except the Oneidas. Occom's influence with the Oneidas was sufficient to secure their neutrality in the war. (44)

Upon Wheelock's death in 1779, the Indian school at Hanover seemed on the point of dissolution. The effects of the war on the attitude of the savages were keenly felt in that Indian pupils ceased to attend the school. (45) Occom was taken care of in his last years by a pension provided by the English philanthropist, John Thornton. (46) He collected the remnants of seven Indian settlements which had survived the Revolution and established them at Brothertown, near Utica, N. Y., where he labored until his death in 1792. (47)

Two years after Sergeant's death at Stockbridge, Mass., Jonathan Edwards took charge of the Indian mission there. The town was inhabited almost entirely by the natives, there being about one hundred and fifty families of them, and only twelve families of white people. The outbreak of the French and Indian War led to considerable trouble in the management of the mission, and soon afterward Edwards was induced to become President of the College of New Jersey. Stephen West had charge of the mission until the outbreak of the Revolution when the work was

(43) David McClure, *Memoirs of the Rev. Eleazar Wheelock*, pp. 16, 17.
(44) W. D. Love, *Samson Occom, passim.*
(45) Chase, *op. cit.*, chap. 6.
(46) *Ibid.*, pp. 60, 61.
(47) McClure, *op. cit.*, p. 44; W. D. Love, *op. cit.*

taken in hand by John Sergeant, a son of the founder of the school. In 1785 Sergeant removed the Indians who remained after the vicissitudes of two wars to New Stockbridge, N. Y., near Occom's village of Brothertown. (48)

Of the Six Nations of Central New York, only the Mohawks and Oneidas had received any attention from the various missionary agencies prior to 1765. In that year Samuel Kirkland, a graduate of the College of New Jersey, undertook a most difficult journey to the home of the Senecas, the most remote tribe of the Iroquois. Finding a mission to them impracticable because of their inaccessibility and their terrible savagery, he decided to confine his labors to the Oneidas. He was supported in his work by the Scotch Society and through an appropriation made from the Indian fund of Harvard College. He was driven from his post during the Revolution, but he returned in 1789 and received a grant of land from the Oneidas for the support of the mission. In 1796, according to the report of Morse and Bellknap to the S. P. C. K., there were 628 Indians at New Stockbridge under Kirkland's care, of whom only eight were listed as pagans, but of the Christian Indians there were reported only thirty-six who might be relied upon to refrain from drunken debauches, and only twenty-five who could be classed as "sober Christians." The vast majority believed in and practiced witchcraft. Their fields, when cultivated at all, were cared for by the women. (49) Such was the lamentable picture of the religious and moral condition of the native Americans after a century and a half of sporadic efforts by missionaries to Christianize them.

No account of Protestant missionary endeavor among the natives of America during the eigtheenth century would be complete which omitted to pay tribute to the zealous labors of the Moravian Brethren of Pennsylvania. This little body of religious refugees from Central Europe had originally come to Georgia

(48)   A. C. Thompson, op. cit., pp. 101-105.
(49)   Missionary Magazine, no. 7, Jan. 16, 1797. (London). Report of Morse and Bellknap to the Society in Scotland for Propagating Christian Knowledge.

in accordance with arrangements made with James Oglethorpe, the founder of the English colony there, but had soon migrated to the Lehigh river region in Eastern Pennsylvania because of difficulties growing out of their refusal to bear arms against the Spaniards in the war which broke out between England and Spain in 1739. Count Zinzendorf, a member of the Moravian Church, who had sheltered the refugees on his estate in Saxony when they had been undergoing persecution earlier in the century, came to the new settlements in 1741 to arrange for missionary enterprises among the neighboring Indians. Like Eliot, Zinzendorf believed the Indians to be the Ten Lost Tribes of Israel. In 1742 he concluded a treaty with the Iroquois and thereby laid the foundation for the Moravian mission. (50)

The most famous of the Moravian missionaries to the Pennsylvania Indians was David Zeisberger. His early labors extending over a period of nearly three decades before 1772 resulted in the conversion of about five hundred savages to the Moravian faith. (51) In that year he and his converts abandoned their mission station at Wyalusing on the Susquehanna and went to Central Ohio. In 1791 the remnant of Christian Indians, one hundred and eighty-four in number, who had survived the devastations of war and disease were forced to go to Canada where they remained for seven years. Returning to Goshen, Ohio, after their exile, the mission Indians gradually disappeared, and, by the time of Zeisberger's death in 1808, it was a foregone conclusion that all further efforts to keep alive the few remaining embers which testified to his zeal for evangelizing the natives would be useless. (52) Forces were at work which rendered futile all the heroism of the pioneer missionary, whether he happen to be John Eliot, David Brainerd, or David Zeisberger. The land hunger of the white settlers, the susceptibility of the

(50)   J. E. Hutton, *A History of Moravian Missions*, pp. 78-116.
(51)   John Woolman, *Journal*, pp. 76-96.
(52)   J. E. Hutton, *op. cit.*; J. H. Livingston, Appendix to sermon delivered before the New York Missionary Society, April 3, 1804; E. R. Hasse, *The Moravians*, chap. 2.

natives to the diseases and the vices of the white man, and, perhaps as significant as either of them, the inability of the Protestant missionaries to adapt their method of appeal to the needs and the understanding of the natives—all these factors serve to explain, in part at least, why Indian missions failed.

CHAPTER II

THE SECOND GREAT AWAKENING

The Great Awakening which is associated with the labors of Jonathan Edwards and George Whitefield had spent its force long before the opening of the Revolution. In many places, especially in New England, it had engendered unpleasant controversies. A schism between the "Old Lights" and the "New Lights" developed. The Old Lights protested against the lack of moderation shown by the revivalists. The New Lights, on the other hand, were incessantly bewailing the lack of piety and religious enthusiasm possessed by their moderate brethren. Presbyterians and Congregationalists suffered the most by reason of the bitterness engendered. In many instances churches were rent by the factional strife. (1)

At the same time, controversies were raging between the orthodox and liberal parties, the latter of which was sometimes confused with the Old Light group because of its criticism of revivalist methods. The Liberals, however, differed from the Old Lights in their attitude toward the cardinal points of Calvinism. Liberalism, which tended to be either Universalist or of a very mild Unitarian variety, centered about Boston, although its influence was diffused pretty much throughout New England and the Middle Colonies. An outstanding Liberal of the Universalist wing was Charles Chauncy of the First Church in Boston. A sermon of Chauncy's, published in London in 1784, caused a considerable stir in religious circles in America and led to a veritable deluge of pamphlets and books, commending or attacking Chauncy's

(1)   H. L. Osgood, *The American Colonies in the Eighteenth Century,* vol. iii, pp. 409-490.

theory of a universal restoration of all mankind as the chief end aimed at by the Creator. (2)   Jonathan Mayhew of the West Church, Boston, was called an Arian because of his interpretation of the doctrine of the Trinity. (3) The first avowedly Unitarian Church in America was King's Chapel which had been Episcopalian but which adopted a Unitarian liturgy shortly after the close of the Revolution. (4) Every liberal tendency was regarded with abhorrence by the followers of Edwards who were coming to be styled Edwardeans to distinguish them from the Old Light Calvinists. Edwardeanism was being further developed along somewhat different lines by Samuel Hopkins, an ardent disciple of Edwards. "Consistent Calvinism" as Hopkins liked to call his system was a militant faith. Willingness to be damned for the glory of God was one of its peculiar tenets. Heroism was required of its followers which would equal, if it did not excel, that shown by the Jesuits. At a later period "Consistent Calvinism" was destined to furnish the dynamic for foreign missions. (5)

The Revolutionary War tended to disrupt religious bodies considerably. The spread of radical philosophical ideas of deistic and atheistic varieties was facilitated through the presence of the English and the French soldiers during the course of the struggle. It was but natural that the recovery of the churches should be slow and that programs of advancement would need to await a more favorable time. Especially destructive was the effect of the war upon the work of the Episcopal establishment. The S. P. G., which had been the more active agency of Anglicanism in the colonies, likewise ceased its operations within the bounds of the United States and confined its work to British colonies. (6) The Episcopal Church itself was all but extin-

(2)   Charles Chauncy, Sermon: "The mystery hid from ages and generations, made manifest by the gospel revelation; or, the Salvation of all men the great Thing aimed at in the Scheme of God. By one who wishes well to the whole human race."

(3)   George W. Cooke, *Unitarianism in America*, p. 63.

(4)   Robert Baird, *Religion in America*, p. 626.

(5)   Williston Walker, *Ten New England Leaders*. Chapter on Samuel Hopkins.

(6)   C. H. Robinson, *The Story of the S. P. G.*, p. 17.

guished in America. Its clergy at the close of the struggle were still nominally subject to the Bishop of London, but the maintenance of such alien oversight was impossible in view of the feelings of the victorious patriots toward everything savoring of Toryism. Under such circumstances Episcopalianism would be more unwelcome in America than Roman Catholism.

It was with a view to finding a remedy for the difficulty created by the outcome of the Revolution that Samuel Seabury was ordained Bishop of the American Episcopal Church at the hands of the Scotch nonjuring Bishops rather than by the episcopate in England. The ordination of Samuel Provoost and William White was made possible in 1787 by special parliamentary legislation permitting the omission of the customary oath of allegiance to the British crown. The First General Convention of the Protestant Episcopal Church of America met in Philadelphia in 1789. It comprised two of the Bishops and twenty other clergymen, along with sixteen laymen. (7) For many years the Episcopal Church was struggling for bare existence and its influence was slight.

At the General Convention of 1792 resolutions were passed to collect a missionary fund. The plan, however, proved premature, and it was finally decided to leave the conduct of missions to the Conventions of the states. In 1809 the Episcopal Church of New York State was supporting three workers through annual collections taken in the churches. (8) It was not until 1816 that the Episcopal Church undertook missionary work among the Indians. In that year Eleazar Williams, the supposed "Lost Dauphin" of France, sought the conversion of the pagan party among the Oneidas. As a result of Williams' labors Bishop Hobart confirmed fifty-six red men of the Oneida tribe on the occasion of the consecration of an Indian Church in 1819. (9)

(7)   Hugh L. Burleson, *The Conquest of the Continent*, pp. 35-38.
(8)   John H. Livingston, Sermon delivered before the New York Missionary Society, April 3, 1804. Appendix.
(9)   *Handbook of the Church's Missions to the Indians*, pp. 85-86.

The denominations which showed the most remarkable development from the close of the Revolution to the period of the Second War with Great Britain were two bodies which prior to 1775 had been regarded as of little importance, namely, the Methodists and the Baptists. The latter along with the Presbyterians and the Congregationalists had, for the most part, shown an intense patriotism during the national struggle. The former, however, owing to their partial connection with the Church of England and through the loyalism of Wesley and some other prominent leaders had suffered the stigma of Toryism. Nevertheless, after the war Methodism developed rapidly.

Methodist societies in England grew up within the Established Church chiefly through the activities of the brothers John and Charles Wesley. The first society was formed in London in 1739, and within a few years Methodism had spread to other parts of the British Isles. Some emigrants from Ireland who had been members of a society there came to New York in 1766 and established the first American Methodist Society with Philip Embury as preacher. In response to an appeal for aid from the New York Methodists Wesley sent over Richard Boardman and Joseph Pillmore to act as missionaries in New York and Philadelphia. In 1771 Francis Asbury arrived, and after that time missionary work was no longer confined to cities. (10)

At the time of Asbury's arrival there were probably not more than six hundred Methodists in all the colonies. Most of them were to be found in New York and Philadelphia. (11) By 1775 their number had been increased to 3,000 and by 1786 to 20,000. (12) The growth of the denomination was phenomenal. In 1807 Asbury calculated the number of Methodists in the United States at 144,590 with 536 traveling preachers and 1,400 other

---

(10)   Nathan Bangs, *History of the Methodist Episcopal Church*, vol. i, pp. 37-70.

(11)   Francis Asbury, *Journal*, vol. iii, p. 109.

(12)   J. M. Buckley, *A History of the Methodists in the United States*, p. 253.

local exhorters. (13)   Asbury himself was said to have preached 16,500 sermons, ordained more than 4,000 preachers, and traveled on horseback and by carriage 270,000 miles. (14)   Writing in his journal towards the close of his life he said:

In the year 1774, I first visited Virginia and North Carolina: in the year 1780, I repeated my visit; and since that time yearly. In the year 1785, I first visited South Carolina and Georgia; and to these states have since paid (except one year) an annual visit until now. [Nov., 1814.] I suppose I have crossed the Alleghany mountains sixty times. (15)

The rapid growth of Methodism in America and the need of some centrally established authority equipped with power to ordain ministers and to direct the work of the societies led to the ordination in 1784, first of Thomas Coke by John Wesley, then of Francis Asbury by Coke, as Superintendents of the Methodist Episcopal Church in America.   This action was taken only after unsuccessful efforts had been made to induce the Bishop of London to ordain a minister for America. (16)   Its irregularity was acknowledged but the action was explained by Methodists as necessary for the proper care of the societies.   Coke and Wesley were both clergymen of the Church of England but were not Bishops.   Asbury allowed himself to be called "Bishop" in spite of Wesley's vigorous protests over the title.

The Methodist hierarchy bore close resemblance to that of its parent the Church of England.   The form of organization, centrally directed as it was, had much to do with the success of the Church. It was admirably adapted to grapple with the problems created by a westward moving population. Missionary enterprises were conducted with a maximum of efficiency because they were centrally administered.   Asbury himself possessed just those

(13)   Asbury, *Journal*, vol. iii, p. 230.
(14)   J. M. Buckley, *Hist. Methodists*, p. 245.
(15)   Asbury, *Journal*, vol. iii, p. 361.
(16)   *Ibid.*, vol. i, pp. 377-378.

traits of self-renunciation and zeal for the cause which were needed to make his subordinates willing to endure hardship without murmuring when ordered. The Methodist circuit riders were expected to obey with the same readiness as that which characterized the Jesuit missionaries. Each pioneer was a soldier of the cross, and every contest with the powers of darkness was a crusade for Methodism.

The early Methodists emphasized evangelism of the most primitive character. The camp-meeting, first used in Kentucky, became the established institution of the Methodists. Asbury remarked that the Methodists were all for camp-meetings just as the Baptists were for public baptizings. (17) He was happy to learn that there would be five hundred camp-meetings during the year 1808. (18) During the period of the Second Great Awakening the Methodists reaped an abundant harvest on the Western frontier through their readiness to make use of the camp-meeting and through the stress they placed on "lowly preaching."

Another advantage of Methodism as a missionary religion was the importance given in their theology to the Arminian doctrine of the freedom of the will. Wesleyan Methodism took exception to the idea of predestination as understood by disciples of Calvin. However, Wesley's followers did not become Universalists as did many of the anti-Calvinists of New England. It was true, they said, that Christ died for all mankind, but, unlike the followers of Chauncy and Winchester, they insisted that the sacrifice made by Christ was inoperative outside the circle of those who accepted it. This took the burden of responsibility from God and placed it squarely upon the shoulders of each individual. To the Methodist convert, then, there was an assurance of salvation which transcended that of the "hopefully pious" Calvinist in whose mind there often lingered considerable uncertainty in the matter. Religious experience was joyful

(17)   *Ibid.*, vol. iii, p. 298.
(18)   *Ibid.*, vol. iii, p. 249.

and at times ecstatic. An emotional explosion released much of the latent energy of the Methodist and enabled him to engage with zeal in the task of saving others and of doing deeds of a benevolent nature. Some Methodists became "perfectionists"; all were stirred with a feeling of buoyant and triumphant optimism.

New England, the stronghold of Calvinism and the Congregational Church, was looked upon by the Methodists as missionary ground. The New Light controversy enabled the Methodists to secure some recruits in an otherwise cold society. Freeborn Garrettson on his way back from Nova Scotia where he had been working in a missionary capacity from 1785 to 1787 made a tour of New England. He found few traces of Methodism, although there were small societies in several of the larger cities like Boston, Providence, and Newport. It remained for Jesse Lee to plant Methodism in New England, beginning in 1789. The missionary character of the New England enterprise was acknowledged in the taking of collections for it in Maryland, Delaware, Pennsylvania, and New York. (19) Within two years Lee had inaugurated permanent societies in every New England State. (20)

The revival which started in New England and spread to the Western and Southwestern parts of the country toward the close of the century was due in no small degree to the evangelistic fervor of the Methodist circuit riders. At Yale College in 1802, when the revival was at its height in that part of New England, the Methodists, according to Asbury, succeeded in making an impression where ridicule had been their lot hitherto. (21) On the frontier no denomination, except possibly the Baptist, followed the pioneer into the howling wilderness with such persistency for the welfare of his soul as did the organization directed by Bishop Asbury. Shortly before his death Asbury wrote in his journal a virtual summary of the Methodist attitude in this re-

(19)   N. Bangs, *op. cit.*, vol. i, pp. 289-318.
(20)   *Ibid.*, vol. ii, p. 16.
(21)   Asbury, *Journal*, vol. iii, p. 66.

spect: "We cannot leave four or five thousand congregations un-sought, like the Church of England, the Presbyterian, Independent, and Baptist Churches. Go, says the command; go into all the world—go to the highways and hedges. Go out—seek them, Christ came seeking the lost sheep." (22)

After General Wayne's Treaty with the Indians in 1795 the population of the Northwest Territory increased rapidly. To the ever-alert Asbury the opportunity to establish a strong religious organization in the sparsely settled regions seemed nothing less than providential. The same methods of organization and development were followed in the new territory as those which had characterized the Methodist movement from the outset. First, it was essential that there be a small Methodist nucleus in a community. Missionary workers would then proceed to the region in order that the religious zeal of the members might be quickened. The next step was the selection of a local exhorter or preacher to look after the flock between the periodical visits of the circuit rider. Then would follow the organization of a full-fledged Methodist society. The migration of a few members of the society or church would serve to constitute a new Methodist nucleus somewhere else. In this way the whole process would be repeated. Methodist growth was indissolubly linked up with incessant missionary activity, centrally directed. In 1804 for instance Benjamin Young was sent as missionary to Illinois. The people among whom he labored were chiefly the descendants of the old French settlers. The following year Young reported sixty-seven members of Methodist societies in Illinois. (23) Elisha Bowman, in like manner, was sent to Louisiana in 1806. (24)

One of the most important fields of missionary labor sought by the imaginative Methodist evangelists was the country to the North and Northeast of the United States. In 1784, the year

(22)   *Ibid.*, p. 367.
(23)   N. Bangs, *op. cit.*, vol. ii, p. 166.
(24)   *Ibid.*, pp. 179-180.

Asbury was made Superintendent of American Methodism, William Black, an English preacher who had succeeded in planting Methodism in Nova Scotia besought his American brethren for aid. Freeborn Garrettson and James Cromwell were sent in response to the appeal and, in a restricted sense, may be regarded as foreign missionaries. William Losee, a member of the New York Conference, visited Upper Canada in 1791 and formed the first society at Kingston. (25) Some Methodists were to be found in the region before Losee arrived, but there was no organization. Ten years after Losee's visit five circuits were in existence with 1,160 Methodists under the care of American clergymen. The most famous of these American circuit riders was Nathan Bangs who in 1804 was sent to organize a new circuit on the River Thames in Upper Canada. After Bangs left Upper Canada to labor in Montreal, William Case, a native of Massachusetts, took charge of the Thames circuit. (26)

The camp-meeting was introduced into Canada in 1805 by Henry Ryan and William Case, and under the leadership of these Americans a revival broke out similar to those under way in the United States at the same time. (27) Under Samuel Coate Methodism was started in Montreal, and Nathan Bangs was made Presiding Elder of Lower Canada, a position he held until the outbreak of the War of 1812, when he returned to the United States to take charge of the Rhinebeck District in New York and Connecticut. At the close of the war, Ryan was in charge of Lower Canada, and Case of Upper Canada. Case was instrumental in the organization in 1822 of a mission among the Indians near the Bay of Quinte. In 1820 Lower Canada was taken over by the British conference as a missionary district. Eight years later Case was made president of an Independent Methodist Conference comprising Upper Canada. (28)

(25)   N. Bangs, *op. cit.,* vol. i, p. 322.
(26)   Abel Stevens, *Life and Times of Nathan Bangs, passim.*
(27)   Findlay and Holdsworth, *The History of the Wesleyan Methodist Missionary Society,* vol. i, pp. 367-369.
(28)   Nathan Bangs, *op. cit.,* vol. ii, p. 385.

There was much in common between Methodists and Baptists despite radical divergences in organization and ritual. Both emphasized lowly preaching, soul saving, and sudden conversion. Both stressed the necessity of conversion as a prerequisite for admission to full church membership. Both denominations were aggressive in pushing out the Christian frontier in America to the very edges of civilization, and even beyond. The necessity of an educated clergy was felt less by these two bodies than by Presbyterians, Congregationalists, and Episcopalians. A larger proportion of the membership of Baptist and Methodist churches was drawn from the elements of American society having the least culture. The rapid growth of these two bodies during the last quarter of the eighteenth century was an important factor in the rise of the missionary spirit because of the dependence of both denominations upon missionary methods for their enlargement.

It is estimated that there were about three hundred Baptist churches in the United States in 1776, with less than ten thousand members. (29)   On the outstanding doctrinal question of the period, that of predestination, the Baptists were not united. The Philadelphia Association which had been formed in 1707 represented the most vigorous group of churches in the denomination.   It comprised at one time churches scattered all the way from New York to South Carolina.   In the Philadelphia Association as originally constituted the predominant principles were Calvinistic, although Methodist influences in the far South led to considerable discussion and dissension.   In New England before the Great Awakening the Baptists were Arminian or "Freewill," for the most part, but the subsequent accession of New Lights to the Baptist fold leavened the churches with Calvinism, and in many instances led to considerable disturbance over doctrines. (30)

(29)   Henry C. Vedder, *A Short History of the Baptists,* p. 210. J. L. Diman, Religion in America (1776-1876), *North American Review,* January, 1876.

(30)   A. H. Newman, *A History of the Baptist Churches in the United States,* pp. 210-330.

Largely as a result of persistent evangelistic efforts the Baptists increased the membership of their churches from less than ten thousand at the period of the Revolution to over a hundred thousand at the close of the century. (31)   At the beginning of the Foreign Missionary movement in America during the second decade of the nineteenth century the total number of Baptists in the seventeen states of the Union numbered 172,972. There were at that time (1812) 2,164 churches under the charge of 1,605 ministers. The three leading Baptist states were Virginia, Kentucky, and New York. There were more Baptists in Virginia in 1812 than in all the New England states. (32)

Farther South the work of the Baptist preachers took on all the characteristics of an African mission. In Georgia one-half of the entire population was comprised of slaves. Baptists and Methodists were foremost in this missionary work. Colored ministers were encouraged by the white leaders to evangelize the pagan blacks. One of the most famous of the early negro Baptist preachers was George Lisle of Savannah; he labored among the slaves during the Revolution, but after the war his master who was a Tory took him to Jamaica. Lisle began what may be styled missionary work in his new home. (33)

One of Lisle's converts in Georgia was Andrew Bryan who labored until his death in 1812 to redeem his fellow slaves from paganism. That his services were not unappreciated by the white people of Georgia was made clear by a minute published by the Savannah Baptist Association after his death, which read:

The Association is sensibly affected by the death of the Rev. Andrew Bryan, a man of color, and pastor of the First Colored Church in Savannah. This son of Africa, after suffering inexpressible persecutions in the cause of his divine Master, was at length permitted to discharge the duties of the ministry among his colored friends in peace and quiet, hundreds of whom, through his instru-

(31)   H. C. Vedder, *op. cit.*, p. 211.
(32)   A. H. Newman, *op. cit.*, p. 379.
(33)   Booker T. Washington, *The Story of the Negro*, vol. i, p. 265.

mentality, were brought to a knowledge of the truth as it is in Jesus. He closed his extensively useful and amazingly luminous course in the lively exercise of faith, and in the joyful hope of a happy immortality. (34)

Meanwhile the Congregational churches in New England were experiencing a remarkable invigoration. The "Second Great Awakening," as the revival movement which began in 1797 is sometimes called, was unabated for a period of over five years. Its center seems to have been Connecticut, although during the months following its beginning revivals were reported from such distant regions as Vermont and Maine. A letter from Edward D. Griffin of New Hartford, Conn., to *The Connecticut Evangelical Magazine* told of a revival which began in his church in 1797 with fifty conversions. (35) During 1798 and 1799 a hundred and fifty towns in New England experienced great religious upheavals. (36) A revival which started in Somers, Conn., in 1797 added to the membership of the church fifty-two within a period of two years. (37) In Torringford, Samuel J. Mills, Jr., a youth soon destined to exert great influence in promoting missionary enterprises, became "hopefully pious" as a result of a revival which began in his father's church in August, 1798. (38) Yale College which since 1795 had been under the protecting wing of its belligerently orthodox president, Timothy Dwight, experienced a memorable revival of evangelical piety during the year 1801-02. Among the converts was a senior who was later to promote the missionary cause as editor of *The Panoplist* and as an officer of the American Board. This youth, Jeremiah Evarts, then twenty years old, was just about to begin the practice of law in New Haven. He became an ardent disciple of Calvin, Edwards, and Hopkins. At the time of his conversion he said he "saw no way

(34)   A. H. Newman, *op. cit.*, p. 331.
(35)   *Conn. Evan. Mag.*, Dec., 1800, Letter X on revivals, from Edw. D. Griffin.
(36)   *Theological Magazine*, June, July, and August, 1798.
(37)   *Conn. Evan. Mag.*, July, 1800.
(38)   *Ibid.*

in which our nation could be saved from infidelity and utter ruin, except by revivals of religion, more numerous and powerful than any heretofore experienced." (39)

During 1798 and 1799 the revival area came to include the settled portions of Maine, towns from all parts of Massachusetts, and quite a number of isolated communities in New York and Vermont. For instance, Jesse Townsend, the Presbyterian minister of Durham, Greene Co., N. Y., told of a revival which had occurred in his little community in the fall of 1799, spurred on by news of similar movements elsewhere, fifty-six members being added to the church. Prayer meetings had preceded the revival. (40) Rev. Aaron Woodworth of Bridgehampton, Long Island, reported one hundred conversions in a revival which lasted from July, 1799, to April, 1800. He accounted for this unusual phenomenon by adding: "In the preceding April, by certain communications, respecting revivals of religion, then taking place in Connecticut and some other concurring circumstances a small number of Christians were induced to set up weekly prayer meetings of special prayer for Zion." (41) These two features, news of revivals from other communities and weekly prayer meetings, seem to have been the usual preliminaries for the spread of the revival to distant towns. The foreign missionary movement was soon to be popularized by two similar agencies, the propaganda of the missionary magazine and the regular weekly prayer meeting.

The Connecticut Missionary Society maintained workers in frontier communities in New York. During 1800 these missionaries reported revivals in Otsego and Delaware Counties. (42) Eliphalet Nott, pastor of the Presbyterian Church at Albany, in a letter to Samuel Miller of New York told of a revival at Bern, a small village in Albany County, where as a result of the religious enthusiasm of the pioneers no less than three churches had

(39)   Gardiner Spring, *Memoir of Jeremiah Evarts*, p. 53.
(40)   *Conn. Evan. Mag.*, June, 1802.
(41)   *Ibid.*, Dec. 1800.
(42)   *Ibid.*, Sept., and Oct., 1800.

appeared. The settlers were people who had emigrated from New England in 1788. A handful of Methodists had maintained a class meeting, but in 1800 there were established regular Baptist, Methodist, and Presbyterian churches. A nearby town had a Dutch Reformed church, which had been established previously. Nott mentioned the considerable attention which was being paid to religion in other parts, specifying Rensselaerville, Coeymans, and Worcester as towns that were coming under the influence of the revival. (43)

Rev. Jedidiah Bushnell, another missionary of the Connecticut Society, reported similar news concerning the Otsego and Delaware region and added that the movement had reached as far west as Ontario County by the close of the year 1800. (44) In a later communication he told of the progress of the movement during 1800 in Vermont, specifying such towns as Cornwall, Middlebury, New Haven, and Waitsfield as having experienced unusual revivals of religion. (45)

At Lebanon, N. Y., a revival occurred during the closing months of 1801. At that time there were but eleven members of the church there. Two sermons by the pastor on the miseries of hell, supplemented by the prayers of the faithful and reports of a great religious awakening in Connecticut and Massachusetts, served to quicken the religious zeal of the ungodly. 140 conversions were reported and the membership of the church increased by 110. The decline of the revival was noted the following March when sectarian controversy arose as a new form of entertainment to replace that afforded by the revival. (46)

Congregationalists, Baptists, and Methodists were by no means the only beneficiaries of the great revival which was sweeping through the older states and into frontier communities during the opening years of the nineteenth century. Every so-

(43)   *New York Miss. Mag.*, 1800, pp. 286-291.
(44)   *Conn. Evan. Mag.*, Sept., 1801.
(45)   *Ibid.*, May, 1802.
(46)   *Conn. Evan. Mag.*, Sept., 1803. Account of Silas Churchill of Lebanon, N. Y.

called evangelical denomination felt the season of refreshing which in some instances did not simply consist of a gentle shower, but must perforce descend with the terrifying violence of a tornado. Particularly was the Presbyterian household of faith invigorated by the Kentucky cyclone, usually known as the Cane Ridge revival.

The General Assembly of the Presbyterian church ever since its first meeting in 1789 had been seeking to extend its frontiers. Radiating out from New York and Philadelphia it had gradually added new synods until by the beginning of the nineteenth century it had jurisdiction over churches in the South and West as well as in the more thinly settled sections of the country.

A report of the proceedings of the General Assembly of the Presbyterian Church, May, 1801, included favorable signs of religious enthusiasm in the Northern and Eastern Presbyteries, but not such encouraging news from the Middle and Southern States. On the borders of Kentucky and Tennessee, however, a great upheaval was in progress. (47)

Two brothers, John and William Magee, the former a Methodist, the latter a Presbyterian, began a preaching tour of Kentucky in 1800. In the course of the great revival which followed, the camp-meeting feature was introduced. (48) Great outbursts of emotionalism were invariable companions of the frontier revivals. At Cane Ridge it was reported that upward of a thousand persons on one occasion were numbered among the "slain." This peculiar phenomenon was but one of the dire effects of the camp meeting. Nervous disorders of almost every description were regarded as evidences of supernatural power at work refuting the bold taunts of the "deistical tribe." Many were reported as having gone to meeting to scoff only to be in turn seized with some weird power and to find themselves tossed about so that seizing on a sapling to support themselves they would wrench

(47)   *Conn. Evan. Mag.*, Aug., 1801.
(48)   *New York Missionary Magazine*, 1802, pp. 85-92; 118-128; 155-160; 175-183. *Conn. Evan. Mag.*, April, June, and Sept., 1802.

the bark loose, or unable to find support would be pitched to the ground, there to lie helpless until the Lord in His mercy granted deliverance. (49)

One result of these unusual occurrences was the renewal of the old controversy among Presbyterians as to the value and desirability of such violent methods of entering the Kingdom of Heaven. People were reminded of an old schism which from 1741 to 1758 had rent the church into two sides over the Whitefield revival. In 1802, however, the General Assembly in its minutes endorsed the revival movement which was going on, but stated that it did not wish to encourage some of its most extravagant accompaniments. (50)   G. A. Baxter, an eye witness of some of the most sensational happenings of the Cane Ridge upheaval, in a letter to Archibald Alexander summarized the movement.

Upon the whole, I think the revival in Kentucky among the most extraordinary that have ever visited the Church of Christ. . . . . Infidelity was triumphant and religion at the point of expiring; something of an extraordinary nature seemed necessary to arrest the attention of a giddy people, who were ready to conclude that Christianity was a fable, and futurity a dream. The revival has done it. (51)

Baxter's opinion was typical of the religious mind of the orthodox leaders at this stirring period when war in Europe threatened not merely to engulf civilization there, but to transfer its mad fury to America as well, and, coupled with Jacobin intrigue and deistical infidelity, to make havoc of all institutions held sacred by Christians. The revival seemed a voice from heaven summoning the faithful to renew their courage, to

---

(49)   *Conn. Evan. Mag.*, Mch., 1802. Letter from G. A. Baxter to A. Alexander. For a thorough study of the Kentucky Revival see Catherine C. Cleveland, *The Great Revival in the West,* 1797-1805.

(50)   *N. Y. Miss. Mag.*, 1802, p. 260; *Ibid.,* July, 1803.

(51)   *N. Y. Miss. Mag.*, 1802, pp. 82-92.

cease defensive tactics, and to assault the enemy all along the line.

These extensive revivals in the Western and Southern Presbyteries dispelled the hitherto prevalent gloom which had characterized the reports made to the General Assembly each year. Much credit was given to the existence of praying societies in communities blessed with revivals of religion. It was noted that special seasons of prayer usually preceded the outbreak of a revival. (52) Excesses such as bodily contortions, regarded as an evidence of the workings of the divine spirit by many, were frowned upon by the sober element among the Presbyterians. Extravagant evangelists were rebuked for encouraging disorderly proceedings. Wild emotionalism was countenanced by but few of the regular clergy in the denomination. (53)

Robert Finley of Baskingridge, N. J., a prominent Presbyterian clergyman who had studied theology under Witherspoon at Princeton, succeeded in bringing about a revival in his community in 1803. As a result of his labors one hundred and twenty persons were taken into the membership of his church, and, according to his account, about three hundred were awakened to the interest of religion. (54) Attributing the revival to the regular prayer circles which had been formed prior to the divine response, Finley retained the regular weekly prayer meeting as a nursery of piety. Through these prayer meetings the missionary spirit was cultivated among the pious. (55) Five years later revivals were reported as flourishing among the young people of Newark, Elizabethtown, and Orangedale. (56) During the year 1807-08 there were added to the churches of the Presbytery of New York 1,120 members. This Presbytery contained twenty-one churches, and the increase which represented an average of fifty-

(52) *Conn. Evan. Mag.,* Aug., 1803.
(53) *Panoplist,* July, 1805, pp. 33-34.
(54) *Mass. Miss. Mag.,* Oct., 1803, p. 238.
    Assembly's Missionary Magazine, July, 1805. Letter from Robert Finley.
(55) I. V. Brown, *Memoir of the Rev. Robert Finley,* p. 63.
(56) *Massachusetts Missionary Magazine,* Jan., 1808.

three members per church was considered unusual. (57) In 1809 there were seven synods in all in the church, comprising thirty-two presbyteries. (58)

Congregational missionaries from New England were engaged in work practically identical in character with that of the Methodist circuit riders and the pioneer evangelists and revivalists. For instance, Joseph Badger, a missionary of the Massachusetts Missionary Society, reported a revival in progress in New Connecticut (the Western Reserve) beginning in October, 1803. (59) Another worker of the same society, Jacob Cram, noted revivals of religion in progress in the course of his journey to New York, Pennsylvania, Ohio, and Canada. In Pennsylvania particularly, the inhabitants he visited were chiefly Presbyterians. He quoted from *The Western Missionary Magazine,* a journal published at Washington, Pa., as follows: "Thus we see in the course of five years a Presbytery consisting of fourteen ministers settled in that country where ten years ago we could scarcely see the face of a white man." In Western New York he reported thirty regular preachers who had come there between 1800 and 1805. There were seven Congregational churches in New Connecticut in 1806 when he made his report. (60)

Meanwhile in New England where the revival movement started it was continuing with renewed vigor in many communities during the first decade of the century. At Plymouth, Mass., the membership of the church doubled as a result of a revival which lasted from March, 1804, to November, 1806. (61) At Williamstown fifty "hopefully pious" and others "anxious," mostly young people, were the fruits of evangelistic preaching which began in May, 1805. Pious parents were encouraged to believe that the younger generation might be saved from the pernicious

(57)   *Panoplist,* Nov., 1808, p. 285;
        Evangelical Intelligencer, Oct., 1808.
(58)   *Evangelical Intelligencer,* June, 1809.
(59)   *Mass. Miss. Mag.,* June, 1805.
(60)   *Ibid.,* Mch., Apr., and May, 1806. Report of Jacob Cram.
(61)   *Ibid.,* Jan., 1807.

fruits of rationalism through the revivals. Convictions of sin were not attended with outcries and other irregular conduct, much to the satisfaction of the conservative people who deprecated such phenomena. (62)

In Vermont a great revival was reported in 1806 by Amos Pettingill, missionary from the New Hampshire Missionary Society. Within the area bounded by Lake Champlain and the Green Mountains, a region one hundred and fifty miles long and about twenty-five miles wide, there were twenty-eight ordained Congregational ministers, all preaching the orthodox tenets. In seventeen churches additions for the five preceding years were twelve hundred and thirty. Several new churches had been set up and the Half-way Covenant was being abolished. Excommunications were more common and church discipline was being stiffened to a noticeable degree. (63)

Attempts to bring about a greater degree of denominational unity among those religious groups which had slight doctrinal divergences were not destined to accomplish much in the way of organic assimilation, but for missionary purposes much was achieved. As early as 1781 the Associate and Reformed Presbyteries united under the name of the Associate Reformed Synod. A working unity of the Associate Reformed, the Dutch Reformed, and the Presbyterian Synods was brought about four years later, but the convention of delegates which was to meet every two years to represent the interests of the three bodies had only advisory power. Even this weak federation was abandoned in 1790. (64)

Nevertheless, beginning in 1791, New England Congregationalists were able to launch a program of interdenominational cooperation with the Presbyterians through arrangements which made possible the attendance at each other's gatherings of delegates from the Connecticut General Association and the Presby-

(62)   *Ibid.,* Oct., 1805.
(63)   *Ibid.,* Oct., 1806.
(64)   William Linn, *Discourses on the Signs of the Times.*

terian General Assembly. After 1794 such delegates were given full voting power reciprocally, and similar arrangements were made between the Massachusetts, Vermont, and New Hampshire Congregational Conventions and the General Assembly. The Plan of Union between the Connecticut General Association and the Presbyterian General Assembly was the outgrowth of these earlier efforts at denominational harmony. (65) The outline of the Plan was the work of the son and namesake of the great Northampton divine, Jonathan Edwards. Agreed upon in 1801, it provided for an accord between Presbyterian and Congregational missionaries on the frontier, so that duplications might be avoided. Arrangements were made whereby Presbyterian ministers might occupy pulpits of churches whose membership was predominantly Congregationalist, and vice versa. It aimed at a closer working unity between the two bodies and no doubt would have led, if it had been followed by similar arrangements in all the New England States, to a merging of the Presbyterian and Congregational denominations. (66) Outside of New England, the Plan worked, for the most part, to the advantage of the Presbyterians, largely because of the directing control of missionary enterprises by the General Assembly. (67)

The growth of interdenominational good-will among those groups not widely separated in doctrine was paralleled by a similar tendency toward cooperation within the denominations. In July, 1802, delegates from various parts of Massachusetts met at Northampton and formed the General Association of Massachusetts proper. Its basis was the "pure principles of Congregationalism." The delegates agreed "to admit as articles of faith the doctrines of Christianity, as they are generally expressed in the

(65)   Williston Walker, *A History of the Congregational Churches in the United States*, pp. 315, 316.

(66)   Acts and Proceedings of the General Assembly of the Presbyterian Church in the United States of America, 1801.

(67)   Albert E. Dunning, *Congregationalists in America*, chap. 17.

Assembly's Shorter Catechism, for the basis of union and fellowship." (68) The objects of the Association as stated were:

> To promote brotherly intercourse and harmony, and their mutual assistance, animation, and usefulness, as ministers of Christ; to obtain religious information relative to the state of their churches, and of the Christian Church in this country, and through the world; and to cooperate with one another and with similar institutions in the most eligible manner for building up the cause of truth and holiness. (69)

Within the Baptist denomination efforts were being made to bring about working unity between the Regular and Separate branches who differed about predestination and free will. The Regulars tended to be extreme Calvinists while the Separates favored Arminianism. These differences were very marked in the Southern states where the Baptists were strongest. In Virginia there had been a rapprochement between the two groups so that by 1787 an agreement was reached whereby all distinctions were ended, (70) The distinction between Regulars and Separates disappeared also in North and South Carolina, (71) although throughout the South the Baptists tended to remain strongly Calvinistic, partly through their contact with the Arminian Methodists.

As a direct result of the planning of the Philadelphia Association the College of Rhode Island (after 1804 Brown University) had been instituted in 1764. It remained for half a century the only degree conferring college under Baptist control. Williams College (1793), Bowdoin (1794), Union (1795) and Middlebury (1800) were founded largely as a result of the desire of the Congregational and Presbyterian churches for an educated ministry. All of these new institutions, as well as older colleges

(68)   *Panoplist,* July, 1807.
(69)   *Mass. Miss. Mag.,* June, 1807.
(70)   A. H. Newman, *Hist. Bap. Chs. in U. S.,* p. 301.
(71)   *Ibid.,* pp. 314-330.

such as Yale and Princeton, were considerably affected by the great revival under way during the decade following 1797. Men destined to become outstanding leaders in the missionary field both at home and abroad were dreaming dreams and seeing visions while students in these colleges.

To the Presbyterian General Assembly of 1809 the situation seemed incomparably more hopeful than it had ten years earlier. Revivals everywhere, additions to the churches, and a decided change in the attitude of people generally toward religious matters were among the hopeful signs noted. Well might pious people rejoice and conclude that the great prophecies were about to find fulfillment in the conversion of the heathen. The annual report on the state of religion concluded with apocalyptic fervor:

We have only to add our ardent prayer, that the angel flying through the midst of heaven, having the everlasting gospel to preach to every kindred and tongue, may soon reach the bounds of his destination; that every obstacle that might impede his flight, or stay his progress, may be speedily removed, and that the knowledge of Christ may soon cover the earth, as the waters cover the sea. (72)

(72)   *Panoplist,* June, 1809.

CHAPTER III

LOCAL SOCIETIES AND EARLY MISSIONARY LITERATURE

The period of the Second Great Awakening of American Christianity was a notable one in the history of missions. In Great Britain and on the continent of Europe a new day was dawning. In 1792 at Kettering, England, the Particular Baptists organized a missionary society and sent William Carey to India. Three years later the London Missionary Society was organized by Independents, Presbyterians, and adherents of the Church of England. The Established Church likewise bestirred itself before the close of the century and launched the Church Missionary Society. In Scotland and in the Netherlands similar movements were under way. Plans were formulated and workers sent out with a view to the ultimate evangelization of the heathen world. Asia, Africa, and the South Sea Islands were no longer to be neglected fields for Protestant missionary endeavor. To some it seemed that the greatest age in the world's history since the days of the apostles had arrived. (1)

It was not until after the Second War with Great Britain that the American states secured anything like economic freedom from Europe. To a much greater degree were religious movements in the new world dependent upon those in the old. It was but natural that Americans should derive encouragement from the organization of the British missionary societies. Methods of organization and propaganda were deliberately borrowed from the London Missionary Society by the New York Missionary

(1) *The Theological Magazine,* 1798, no. 1. Introduction.

Society which was initiated in 1796. (2)   The American Board of Commissioners for Foreign Missions assumed the responsibility of caring for its first missionaries to Asia only after Judson had unsuccessfully sought aid from the London Society. (3)   In like manner the New York Bible Society made an unsuccessful appeal for aid from the British and Foreign Bible Society shortly before the organization of the American Bible Society in 1816. (4)   American Christians, whether Anglicans, Methodists, Presbyterians, Congregationalists, or Baptists, all felt a sense of dependance upon their brethren across the Atlantic.

Nevertheless, after making full allowance for all the evidences of American religious dependency upon Europe, there were not wanting signs that the Christian bodies of the New World were becoming increasingly conscious of a sense of responsibility for the evangelization of mankind.   Due in part to the spirit of a slowly developing nationalism there was evident a feeling of friendly rivalry which was suggesting that Americans ought to emulate their British brethren in their zeal for missions. The first effect of the newly awakened missionary enthusiasm was an increased activity on the part of churches and associations in Indian missionary work.   Then migration on a large scale from New England, especially from Connecticut to Vermont, New York, and Ohio, which had begun after 1763, and which was greatly stimulated by the Treaty of 1783, awakened the Congregational Churches in New England to the need of missionary endeavor among the frontier settlers.   The virtual failure of the Indian missions and the tendency of new settlements to become religiously self-supporting after a few years contributed to an enlargement of the missionary horizon and ultimately led to the launching of missions in the Far East.   In the meantime, the organization of voluntary missionary societies, the collection

(2)   *U. S. Christian Magazine,* 1796, no. 2, p. 149; *New York Missionary Magazine,* 1802, p. 6. Address of the London Missionary Society, May 18, 1802; *N. Y. Miss. Magazine,* Oct., 1803.

(3)   Edward Judson, *Life of Adoniram Judson,* p. 25.

(4)   Gardiner Spring, *Memoir of Samuel J. Mills,* pp. 89, *et seq.*

of money, and the launching of missionary journals, all testified to the significance attached to the evangelization of the frontier and the wilderness. The first of these voluntary societies to appear was the Society for Propagating the Gospel among the Indians and Others in North America.

In 1762 an attempt was made by a number of citizens of Boston to establish a Society for the Promotion of Christian Knowledge on the plan of the Society in Scotland for Propagating Christian Knowledge. The Archbishop of Canterbury disapproved of the measure on the ground that it would interfere with the Society for the Propagation of the Gospel in Foreign Parts, the missionary agency of the Anglican Church. In consequence the organization of the society was deferred for a quarter of a century until political independence had been secured. In 1787 the American Society for Propagating the Gospel among the Indians and Others in North America was given legal status through an act of the Massachusetts Legislature. A separate fund for the work among the Indians was made possible through the John Alvord endowment. (See below) Financial aid was furnished to the aged Zechariah Mayhew of Martha's Vineyard, Gideon Hawley of Marshpee, and John Sergeant of New Stockbridge. (5) When Mayhew died in 1806, there were but 212 Indians left at Martha's Vineyard. The mission was then placed in the care of two old Indians named Hansuit and Jeffer. Hawley's mission at Marshpee comprised about fifty Indians who owned several thousand acres of land. (6)

In 1809 an agreement was made between the Society for Propagating the Gospel and the Harvard College corporation whereby the Marshpee and Vineyard Indians would be under the sole care of the latter, while the former would be responsible

(5)   *Theological Magazine*, March, April, and May, 1798.
      New York Missionary Magazine, 1800, pp. 427-433; *Mass. Miss. Mag.*, Mch., 1806.
(6)   *Panoplist*, Dec., 1806.

for the salary of Sergeant at New Stockbridge. (7) Other Indian missions of the Society for Propagating the Gospel were
instituted among the remnants of the Narragansett tribe, living
at Charlestown, R. I., and among the Wyandot Indians near Sandusky, Ohio. Of the Narragansetts only about one hundred and
fifty remained. They had first been evangelized by Whitefield,
Davenport, and other "New Lights" during the period of the
Great Awakening. The Society for Propagating the Gospel and
the Rhode Island Missionary Society assumed financial responsibility for the erection of a school building, and the Society for
Propagating the Gospel employed a schoolmaster. In 1809 one
hundred dollars was sent by the S. P. G. to aid Joseph Badger
in his work among the Wyandots of Ohio. (8) In addition to its
Indian teachers the Society employed workers to evangelize the
white settlers in Maine. In 1806 four such missionaries were
laboring on the frontier. (9) By 1812 the number had been increased to ten. (10)

The original collection of $1,561.01 which had been secured
through the authorization of the Massachusetts Legislature was
inadequate for the work planned by the Society for Propagating
the Gospel. Private subscriptions were therefore resorted to,
and by 1803 a permanent fund of over $23,000 was secured.
Chief among the benefactions was the bequest of Colonel John
Alvord of Charlestown who had died prior to the organization
of the Society, leaving his estate to be given to some organization which would labor for the evangelization of the Indians. His
executor, Richard Cary, transferred the Alvord fund to the S. P.
G. The income from it, over $400 a year, was set apart for the
exclusive purpose of the Indian missions. The remaining in-

(7)　*Missionary Magazine*, no. 7, Jan. 16, 1797, (London); J.
　　　Morse, Sermon before Society for Propagating the Gospel, Nov.,
　　　1810. Appendix.
(8)　*Ibid.*
(9)　*Panoplist*, Dec., 1806.
(10)　*Society for Propagating the Gospel among the Indians and Oth-
　　　ers in North America.* Anonymous publication.

come of the permanent fund was used for the purchase and distribution of school books, tracts, Bibles, testaments, psalms, and hymns for settlers and aborigines. In the case of the Indians, they were supplied not only with devotional literature, but also with plows, chains, and hoes. The Society believed that little could be done for the natives until they had acquired settled habits of industry. (11)

In view of the rapid extermination of the Indians in New England the trustees of the Society for Propagating the Gospel, in 1812, commissioned Samuel J. Mills and John F. Schermerhorn to make a journey in order to secure exact information about remote tribes of Indians, with the purpose of establishing missions among them. (12) Missionary work, however, was not undertaken by the Society for Propagating the Gospel, among the Western Indians, because in 1816 the American Board of Commissioners for Foreign Missions began to direct its attention to them.

INTERDENOMINATIONAL SOCIETIES IN THE STATE OF NEW YORK

The New York Missionary Society has the distinction of being the first voluntary interdenominational organization of a missionary character in the United States. It was formed September 21, 1796, by a group of ministers and laymen of New York City, chiefly of the Presbyterian, Associate Reformed, Reformed Dutch, and Baptist denominations. Its immediate object was the conversion of the Indians. (13) The first Indians to receive the attention of the Society were the Chickasaws of Georgia and Tennessee. (14) Joseph Bullen and Ebenezer Rice were sent

(11)   *Mass. Hist. Soc. Coll.,* vol. ii, New Series. Sketch of the Society for Propagating the Gospel. (Boston, 1814); *Panoplist,* Feb., 1809.

(12)   *Collections of the Mass. Hist. Soc.,* vol. ii, New Series. Report of J. F. Schermerhorn.

(13)   *N. Y. Miss. Mag.,* 1800, pp. 262-264; 1801, pp. 401-404; Oct., 1803; *U. S. Christian Mag.,* 1796, no. 2, p. 149.

(14)   *Assembly's Missionary Magazine,* March, 1805.

to them in 1799 and instituted a short-lived mission, impractical because it was too far from its base of operations. (15)   It was believed that the Indian tribes of New York State constituted a more opportune field for missionary endeavor.

The New York Baptist Association in 1796 gave favorable consideration to a proposal of Elkanah Holmes, a Baptist minister, that some effort should be made to start a mission among the Tuscarora and Seneca Indians located near Niagara Falls. As the Baptists felt unable to finance such a mission alone their Association prevailed upon the Missionary Society in 1800 to employ Holmes as its agent to the two Indian tribes. (16)   The mission proved to be satisfactory. It was the one Indian enterprise that the New York Society maintained until it turned over its work to the United Foreign Missionary Society in 1821. Although Holmes occasionally made visits to other remote tribes in the region of Lake Erie, he had two regular stations, the Tuscarora, near the Falls of Niagara, and the Seneca, near the site of the present city of Buffalo. (17)   He was more successful in his labors with the Tuscaroras than with the Senecas. The latter were under the influence of Red Jacket, a chief opposed to missions on the ground that Christian Indians were always the first to be exterminated. (18)   Holmes continued in the employ of the Society until two years after the schism between the Baptists and Pedobaptists in the Society which occurred in 1806. It was but natural that the question of the method of administering baptism to the Indian converts should sooner or later cause dissension. The Indian mission was continued, however, by the New York Missionary Society after the Baptists withdrew. (19)

Other Indians who received the attention of the New York Missionary Society were the Catawbas of South Carolina and

(15)   *Ibid.;* Sermon by J. H. Livingston, Apr. 23, 1799, charge by Rodgers to Bullen, *N. Y. Miss. Mag.,* 1801, pp. 401-404.

(16)   *N. Y. Miss. Mag.,* 1800, pp. 292-293; *Pan.,* Oct., 1805, p. 227; *Pan.,* Jan., 1807.

(17)   *N. Y. Miss Mag.,* June, 1803.

(18)   *Assembly's Miss. Mag.,* March, 1805.

(19)   *Mass. Baptist Miss. Mag.,* Sept., 1810, pp. 328-332.

the remnants of various tribes, located in Suffolk County, L. I. Paul Cuffee, a native of Elizabeth Island, later to be prominent in the movement for the colonization of free negroes, was employed by the Society at a salary of eighty dollars a year to labor among the few remaining Indians near his home. (20)

Two auxiliary societies were begun in 1809 to assist the New York Missionary Society in financing its Indian enterprises. The first was known as the Young Men's Missionary Society of New York, an interdenominational affair, which seven years later separated from the parent organization and undertook missionary enterprises of its own. The second was the Presbyterian Youth's Assistant Missionary Society. (21)

The receipts of the New York Missionary Society increased from $1,000 in 1800 to nearly $5,000 in 1803. The Chickasaw mission required nearly all the income of the Society at the outset, but after it was abandoned the various stations in New York were reinforced by additional workers. (22)

A missionary society closely allied with, yet never organically a part of, the New York Missionary Society was started in Lansingburgh, New York, January 11, 1797. It was called the Northern Missionary Society in the State of New York. It was composed of ministers and others interested in propagating the gospel among the Indians, without regard to denominational affiliations. Its avowed purpose was, "to propagate the gospel among the Indian tribes, and in those places of our country which are destitute of its ordinances, and which have not yet organized into Christian Societies." Among the towns represented at its formation were Schenectady, Albany, Salem, Saratoga, Charlton, Troy, Lansingburgh, and Waterford. A conference between some members of the society and the chief of the Oneida Indians was held at Albany, March 13, 1798, and, as a result, four hundred

(20) *N. Y. Miss. Mag.*, 1800, pp. 11, 12; June, 1803, Report of the Directors of the N. Y. Miss. Society, Apr. 4, 1803; Appendix to Livingston's sermon, Apr. 3, 1804.

(21) *Pan.*, May, 1810; G. Spring, *A Brief View of Facts, etc.*

(22) *N. Y. Miss. Mag.*, 1800, p. 165; June, 1803.

acres of land were ceded to the Society by the tribe to support a mission. Legislative assent was secured and the work was begun under a minister and a schoolmaster employed by the Society. (23)

Agents of the societies which were seeking to convert the Indians of Central New York to Christianity reported a formidable obstacle to their enterprise in the influence of the Allegheny Prophet, the brother of the warrior Tecumseh. His influence was most effective among the Onondagas, a tribe located thirty-six miles west of the New Stockbridge mission station. The Prophet sought to prevent his followers from hearing the missionaries but advised the keeping of the Sabbath and living an upright life. Those Indians who were most completely under his sway were anxious to have schools established where their children could receive elementary instruction but with religious teaching excluded. (24)   It was soon recognized by the Society itself that in its work among the Tuscaroras of Central New York, seven-eighths of whom were reported as attached to the missionaries and nominally Christian, (25) the only success of the mission worthy of the name was that attained through the schools. By 1810 the Lancastrian plan of education had been adopted as the most effective way of instructing the Indian children. (26)   The Indian missions of the Northern Missionary Society were continued until 1823, when they were turned over to the United Foreign Missionary Society. (27)

The most important of the many short-lived religious journals which appeared during the closing decade of the eighteenth century was *The Theological Magazine*, published in New York. It was a bi-monthly magazine devoted to discussions of religious

(23)   *N. Y. Miss. Mag.,* 1800, pp. 89-97; A. Green, *Presbyterian Missions,* p. 31.
(24)   *Vt. Evan. Mag.,* March, 1809;
        Mass. Bap. Miss, Mag., June, 1812.
(25)   William Collins, Sermon, May 28, 1806.
(26)   *Pan.,* May, 1810.
(27)   A. Green, *Presbyterian Missions,* p. 31.

questions of various sorts. It included considerable material taken from European sources. Missionary enterprises which were beginning to arouse British Christians were given publicity in *The Theological Magazine.* (28)   A similar journal was issued in New York in 1796, known as *The United States Christian Magazine.* Its aim was "to explain and support the doctrines of the Reformation, to detect and refute error, and to promote vital, practical piety." (29)   In the second issue, missionary intelligence, similar to that which was appearing in *The Theological Magazine* was introduced. Only three numbers of *The Christian Magazine* were published.

In the year 1800 two journals appeared which may properly be regarded as the first American missionary magazines. They were *The New York Missionary Magazine and Repository of Religious Intelligence* and *The Connecticut Evangelical Magazine.* The New York enterprise was destined to have a short career. It gave as its reason for existence the fact that there was no religious intelligence publication in the United States at the date of its first appearance, *The Theological Magazine* having been discontinued the year before. (30)   Much of the material published in *The New York Missionary Magazine* was of British origin. Such publications as *The London Evangelical Magazine, The Edinburgh Missionary Magazine, The Biblical Magazine,* and *The Christian Observer* were freely drawn upon for the purpose of enlightening the American public on missions. (31)   During the first year there were 2,349 subscribers, (32) but in 1803 the publishers decided to discontinue it because of diminished circulation and the failure of its subscribers to pay promptly. (33) Then by 1803 there were two Massachusetts missionary maga-

(28)   *Theological Magazine,* July, 1795-Feb., 1799.
(29)   *U. S. Christian Magazine,* 1796.   Intro., p. 1
(30)   *N. Y. Miss. Mag.,* 1800.   Introduction.
(31)   *N. Y. Miss. Mag.,* Dec., 1803.
(32)   *N. Y. Miss. Mag.,* 1800.   Introduction.
(33)   *N. Y. Miss. Mag.,* Dec., 1803.

zines and one in Connecticut which were competing with the New York journal and which made the continued circulation of the latter unnecessary.

CONGREGATIONAL MISSIONARY SOCIETIES IN NEW ENGLAND

1. CONNECTICUT MISSIONARY SOCIETY

Before the outbreak of the Revolutionary War the Congregational churches in Connecticut were being awakened to the need of missionary endeavor among "the settlements now forming in the wilderness to the westward and northwestward." (34) In 1774 and 1775 the General Association of Connecticut voted to raise funds and send missionaries to some of the pioneer settlements, but these early efforts came to naught because of the war which followed. By 1793, however, there were eight workers in the pay of the Association. The Northern and Western settlers by that time were asking for permanent ministers, and contributions for the purpose of providing settled pastors on the frontier were authorized by the State Legislature in 1792, upon the petition of the General Association. The extension of the frontier work, due in part to the religious awakening of the period, resulted in a call issued June 22, 1797, by the Association for the formation of a voluntary society. The Missionary Society of Connecticut, organized at Hebron, June 21, 1798, was the outcome. (35)

The avowed purpose of the new society, the first of its kind among the Congregationalists of New England, was "to Christianize the Heathen in North America, and to support and promote Christian knowledge in the new settlements within the United States." (36) Delegates from the General Association and one representative from the Presbyterian General Assembly, Samuel

---

(34) Williston Walker, *History of the Congregational Churches in United States*, p. 311.

(35) *Theological Magazine*, April, and May, 1798;
       New York Missionary Magazine, 1800, pp. 170-172.

(36) *Conn. Evan. Magazine*, July, 1800, p. 14.

Miller of New York, comprised the Society. Six clergymen and six laymen made up the Board of Trustees. A charter of incorporation was secured in 1802 which made it possible for the Society to hold property not in excess of $100,000. The profits of *The Connecticut Evangelical Magazine,* the official journal of the organization, were turned over to the trustees for the furtherance of missions. (37)

The earliest workers of the Connecticut Society were sent to Central New York, the Lake George region, Vermont, Delaware and Tioga counties in New York, and Northern Pennsylvania. (38) Joseph Badger went to Ohio in 1800. David Bacon arrived there in 1804, after the Society had decided to abandon its Indian mission. (39)

It was David Bacon who made the only attempt on behalf of the Connecticut Society to establish an Indian mission. Influenced as by magic through reading Edwards's *Life of Brainerd* he traversed the wilderness, journeying on foot in 1800 from Hartford to the region near Lake Erie, inhabited by the remnants of several Indian tribes, and returned with his report later in the year. The following year he sought unsuccessfully to found a mission among the Chippewas near Lake Michigan. The influence of the powwows or conjurers was too strong to overcome. Their argument was that Christian Indians always came to harm. The Moravian Indians were cited as an illustration. The Society decided that an Indian mission would be unwise in view of the opposition encountered and the great outlay required for schools and industrial equipment. Joseph Badger was employed to make a visit to the Wyandot Indians in Ohio but no mission was established then. A few years later, Badger, as agent of the Western Missionary Society, a Presbyterian organization, succeeded in founding one. The Connecticut Society

(37)   Horace Hooker, *Congregational Home Missions in Connecticut.*
(38)   *N. Y. Missionary Magazine,* 1800, pp. 170-172.
(39)   Cornelius Dickinson, *Hist. of Congregationalism in Ohio before* 1852.

in 1809 contributed $100 to assist Badger, but beyond isolated efforts of that sort no other Indian work was attempted. (40)

The trustees' report for 1801 recommended a closer cooperation with other societies which were doing frontier work for the purpose of preventing a disproportionate number of missions being established in a few parts of the country at the expense of destitute regions. The Society for Propagating the Gospel was the first society to send a favorable reply to the request of their Connecticut brethren relative to a plan to avoid the overlapping of their missionary projects. (41)

The first organization to appear as an auxiliary to the Connecticut Missionary Society was the Charitable Female Association of Litchfield, which recommended in 1804 that its members each agree to pay fifty cents a year to the trustees of the Missionary Society. This plan was already finding favor in Boston and in Hampshire County, Mass., in connection with the work of local societies. (42)

The Missionary Society of Connecticut was the strongest of the early voluntary organizations. The treasurer's report for January, 1800, showed contributions and donations of $3,126.88 with disbursements of $883.06. (43)   The following year the total receipts were nearly $3,000, (44) and for 1801 the income of the society including donations, contributions, and interest on funds was over $4,500. (45)   As only a part of the income was spent each year, the surplus in the treasurer's hands piled up until by January 1, 1803 the society was in possession of nearly $10,000, (46) and by 1804 of over $14,000. (47)

(40)   *Conn. Evan. Mag.*, Nov., and Dec., 1801; March, July, and Oct.; 1802; Leonard Bacon, *Historical Discourses*, pp. 56-57; Horace Hooker, *Congregational Home Missions in Connecticut.*
(41)   *Conn. Evan. Mag.*, Aug., 1801.
(42)   *Conn. Evan. Mag.*, Oct., 1804.
(43)   *N. Y. Miss. Mag.*, 1800, p. 182.
(44)   *Conn. Evan. Mag.*, June, 1801.
(45)   *N. Y. Miss. Mag.*, 1802, p. 469; *Conn. Evan. Mag.*, April, 1802.
(46)   *Conn. Evan. Mag.*, March, 1803; *N. Y. Miss. Mag.*, June, 1803.
(47)   *Conn. Evan. Mag.*, April, 1804.

The permanent fund of the society was constantly augment-
ing. In 1801 it was about $1,200, but within three years
it had increased to nearly $7,500. (48) The profits accruing
from the sale of *The Connecticut Evangelical Magazine,* the official organ of the Missionary Society, were turned over to help
swell the permanent fund. During the first year of its appearance 39,192 copies of the magazine were printed at a cost of
$2,605.03. As receipts from the sales of the journal exceeded
the cost of printing by $1,759.60, $1,000 of that amount was
paid to the Trustees of the missionary society on July 8, 1801.
(49) During the first ten years of its existence the Connecticut
Missionary Society did not increase its annual appropriations for
the work of its missions in any way proportionate to the augmentation of its resources. For instance, it paid out for the year
1800 a little over $1,100 and for 1806 a little over $1,250.
(50) The largest amount paid out (prior to 1807) was in 1805
when over $2,500 was spent. (51) By 1806 there was report-
ed a balance on hand of over $21,000, of which nearly $13,000
was the permanent fund, (52) and by 1807 the treasurer
had in his charge over $25,000, including a permanent fund
of over $15,000. (53)

The Connecticut Evangelical Magazine was destined to sur-
vive until after the successful launching of American Foreign
Missions. The first number appeared in Hartford, Conn., in
July, 1800. A minimum of 400 subscribers was required for the
success of the journal. The price of a monthly issue was twelve
and a half cents to subscribers and fourteen cents to others. The
profits were devoted to form a permanent fund, the annual in-

---

(48) *Conn. Evan. Mag.,* Aug. 1801, and April, 1804.
(49) *Conn. Evan. Mag.,* Aug., 1801.
(50) *N. Y. Miss. Mag.,* 1801., p. 338; *Conn. Evan. Mag.,* March,
        1807.
(51) *Conn. Evan. Mag.,* March, 1806.
(52) *Ibid.*
(53) *Conn. Evan. Mag.,* March, 1807.

terest of which was appropriated by the Trustees of the Connecticut Missionary Society to the support of missions in the new American settlements and among the heathen. Justification for the launching of missionary literature was not difficult. "The usefulness of periodical religious publications hath been long experienced in the Christian countries of Europe." National pride also played its part, as according to the editor, "There is also in the public mind a growing confidence in the abilities of American writers and divines to equal their European brethren in evangelical diffusion." (54) The avowed objects of the journal were clearly, if quaintly, summarized after the magazine had passed its first birthday:

> To communicate instruction upon the great truths and doctrines of religion, to comfort and edify the people of God, and to interest the pious mind by exhibiting displays of the grace and mercy of God, rather than to amuse the speculatist and entertain the curious, are the objects of this work. For the accomplishment of these purposes, it will be seen that Essays written in a short, interesting manner, judicious narratives of revivals of religion, accounts of remarkable Providences, and biographical sketches are better adapted, than labored disquisitions on speculative points. (55)

The magazine was discontinued in 1814.

2. BERKSHIRE AND COLUMBIA MISSIONARY SOCIETY

In 1798 there was formed the Congregational Missionary Society in the Counties of Berkshire, [Mass.], and Columbia, [N. Y.]. It was organized by twenty ministers from the two counties, and in its early years sent missionaries to the remote parts of Vermont, New York, Pennsylvania, and Ohio. (56) During the first three years of its existence thirteen workers were in its employ. They served for limited periods, however, and the total

(54)   Conn. Evan. Mag., July, 1800, pp. 4, 5.
(55)   Conn. Evan. Mag., July, 1801, preface.
(56)   N. Y. Miss. Mag., 1802, pp. 401-404; Pan., Feb., 1806.

cost of operations was under $500 for the period 1798-1801. Collections for the same period were a bit under $700. (57) For the following three years (1801-1804) receipts were over $1,200 and disbursements over $850. (58) During the year 1804-1805 as much was received and paid out as had been collected and disbursed during the entire three-year period previous. (59) The expenses of the frontier missionaries for 1804-1805 amounted, however, to only $386.33, and toward this amount the inhabitants of the regions supplied contributed $125.59. (60)

After 1805 the Berkshire and Columbia Society curtailed its operations. From 1806 to 1808 nine missionaries were employed in Vermont and New York and in Berkshire County, Mass. (61) The annual report for the year 1808-1809 showed under $200 collected and a trifle over $250 expended. (62) Seven missionaries were working for the Society in 1808. (63) The chief reason for the decline of the Berkshire and Columbia Society seems to have been the rapid growth of the Connecticut and Massachusetts Missionary Societies which were engaging in pioneer work in the same regions supplied by missionaries of the former. The Society had no missionary magazine.

3. MASSACHUSETTS MISSIONARY SOCIETY

The Massachusetts Missionary Society was established at Boston, May 28, 1799, with the avowed object of diffusing "the knowledge of the gospel among the Heathens, as well as other people in the remote parts of our country, where Christ is seldom or never preached." (64) There were thirty-eight members at the outset, but no missionaries were employed the first year.

(57)   *Conn. Evan. Mag.*, Nov., 1802.
(58)   *Conn. Evan. Mag.*, Dec., 1804.
(59)   *Conn. Evan. Mag.*, Dec., 1805.
(60)   *Pan.*, Feb., 1806, pp. 418, 419.
(61)   *Pan.*, April, 1808.
(62)   *Pan.*, Dec., 1809.
(63)   *Pan.*, March, 1809.
(64)   *N. Y. Miss. Mag.*, 1800, pp. 261-268; *Conn. Evan. Mag.*, March, 1801, p. 352.

(65) It seemed proper for those interested in the propagation of Christianity to "ask when there is so much zeal on the part of wickedness, infidelity and atheism, counteracting the gospel, there be not reason for us to put forth every exertion, for the spread of that precious gospel which is the grand charter of our eternal inheritance." (66)

The militant character of the Missionary Society was but natural in view of the Edwardean or Hopkinsian inclinations of its members. In a letter to Andrew Fuller in 1799, Hopkins asserted that both the Massachusetts and Connecticut Missionary Societies were controlled by Edwardean trustees. (67)

At the second meeting of the Society, May 23, 1801, a membership of 119 and a fund of over $1,000 were reported. (68) The first Missionaries sent out were Jacob Cram and David Avery who went to the sparsely settled region between Whitestown and the Genessee River in New York. (69) The following year (1802) four workers were employed, the two above mentioned, and one each in Maine and Vermont. (70) In 1803 the membership was increased to 240 and a magazine was launched by the Society to assist in propagating orthodox Hopkinsian Christianity at home and abroad. (71) Jacob Cram, who was later (1807) employed by the Northern Missionary Society of New York, reported progress in his work among the Tuscaroras. (72) The chief of the tribe was led to make the astute observation that "white people attend to the gospel and are prosperous; Indians have not attended to it and are diminished, hence they must now attend." (73) By 1809 the Massachusetts Missionary Society had in its employ ten full-time missionaries working among

(65) *Mass. Miss. Mag.,* June, 1803; *N. Y. Miss. Mag.,* Aug., 1803.
(66) *N. Y. Miss. Mag.,* 1801, p. 265.
(67) Samuel Hopkins, *Works,* vol. i, p. 236.
(68) *Mass. Miss. Mag.,* June, 1803; *N. Y. Miss. Mag.,* Aug. 1803.
(69) *Conn. Evan. Mag.,* March, 1801.
(70) *Mass. Miss. Mag.,* June, 1803.
(71) *Mass. Miss. Mag.,* May and June, 1803.
(72) *Mass. Miss. Mag.,* June, 1803.
(73) *Vermont Evan. Mag.,* March, 1809.

pioneers and Indians from Nova Scotia to the settlements of the Wyandots in Ohio. (74)

A modification of the constitution was made in 1804 so that the Massachusetts Missionary Society became, potentially at least, a foreign missionary organization. Its object, as stated in the revised charter, was "to diffuse the Gospel among the people of the newly-settled and remote parts of our country—among the Indians of the country, and through more distant regions of the earth, as circumstances shall invite and the ability of the society shall admit." (75)

The Boston Female Society for Promoting the Diffusion of Christian Knowledge was designed to aid the Massachusetts Missionary Society through purchasing books for distribution to the poor. It comprised at the outset "fourteen pious, praying females." (76) Its constitution adopted in 1801 provided that "no more shall be required of any member than one shilling a month." However, those who wished were at liberty to contribute as much as they thought "consistent with duty." (77)

Another women's auxiliary organization was the "Cent Institution," comprised of Boston women who agreed to pay one cent a week for the purpose of "purchasing Bibles, Dr. Watts' Psalms and Hymns, Primers, Catechisms, Divine Songs, Tokens for Children, etc." for distribution through the workers of the Massachusetts Missionary Society. (78) From June, 1803, to June, 1804, the Cent Institution received $500 for this purpose. Between 1802 and 1808, it collected over $2,000. (79) An appeal to "the Friends of Religion," issued in 1804, was designed to arouse the latent missionary zeal of the women of Eastern Massachusetts. It read:

(74)   *Panoplist, June, 1809; Vermont Evan. Mag., Aug., 1809.*
(75)   *Historical Sketch of the A, B, C, for F. M., pp. 4, 5.*
(76)   *American Baptist Magazine, Nov., 1818.*
(77)   *N. Y. Miss. Mag., 1801, pp. 379-381.*
(78)   *Mass. Miss. Mag., June, 1804, p. 41.*
(79)   *Panoplist, Aug., 1808, p. 41.*

A single cent, when millions are necessary to carry into effect the benevolent designs of our Fathers and Brethren, who are engaged in sending the gospel to lands unenlightened with its genial rays, may appear at first view, small and inconsiderable. :— But, should the Friends of Zion adopt the Plan of Contributing one cent a week and recommend the same practice to their friends and connections; it is presumed a very handsome sum may be annually collected, without inconvenience to individuals.... Mrs. John Simpkins requests those who are disposed to encourage this work to send in their names, with their money, quarterly, or as shall be most agreeable to them;— and she will engage to deposit it with the Treasurer of the Massachusetts Missionary Society for the important purpose of aiding that very laudable Institution.... The ocean is supplied by rivers, made up of small streams. Remember the widow's two mites." (80)

The methods of the Cent Institution became famous not only in New England where it originated but also in Great Britain. *The London Evangelical Intelligencer,* the leading missionary magazine in the British Isles, sought to have the women's mite societies reproduced there. "Were such a method adopted in England, among the females of all religious congregations, and devoted by a committee of each society to the missionary cause, or to any other institutions intended to promote the good of souls, what a vast sum might be accumulated without inconvenience to individuals." (81)

Aided by the zeal of the women and by the rising tide of interest in European missions to the Far East and among the South Sea Islanders the Massachusetts Missionary Society began from its very outset a prosperous career. Over $1,000 came into the treasury to be disbursed for the year 1802-03. (82) For the year ending May, 1806, collections and donations amounted

(80)   *Mass. Miss. Mag.,* June, 1804, p. 41.
(81)   *Mass. Miss. Mag.,* June, 1806, Reprint from *London Evan. Mag.*
(82)   *Mass. Miss. Mag.,* June, 1803, pp. 73-75.

to over $2,300. (83)   Nearly $4,000 was received and under $2,000 expended from May, 1806, to May, 1807. (84)

The president of the Massachusetts Missionary Society during its early years was Nathaniel Emmons, a disciple of Samuel Hopkins. (85)   The magazine of the Society was issued monthly at Salem.   The editors, thirteen in number, at the outset included such prominent clergymen as Nathaniel Emmons, Samuel Spring, Abiel Holmes, Samuel Worcester, and Elijah Parish. *The Massachusetts Missionary Magazine* was run at a profit from its beginning in 1803. (86)   In 1804-1805 its directors turned over $400 to the Missionary Society in addition to 6,600 copies of the magazine for gratuitous distribution at the hands of the missionaries. (87)

In 1805 Jedidiah Morse launched another religious magazine known as *The Panoplist*.   The reasons for founding this journal were, according to a later statement by its editor, that the importance of the Christian cause made it necessary to contend for the faith once delivered to the saints and that alarming events in Europe and America were encouraging the enemies of the gospel to believe that the moral and social order might be speedily overthrown.   For these reasons those who were backing *The Panoplist* wished to expose New England Unitarianism as nothing but infidelity in disguise. (88)   The controversy engendered over the election of a successor to Dr. Tappan for the Hollis professorship of Divinity at Harvard College had convinced Morse and some other "moderate" Calvinists that all distinctions between Hopkinsians and Old Calvinists might well be forgotten in view of the greater controversy raging between orthodox and liberal factions.   From the time *The Panoplist* was launched

(83)   *Mass. Miss. Mag.,* June and August, 1806.
(84)   *Mass. Miss. Mag.,* July, 1807.
(85)   *Panoplist,* June, 1808.
(86)   *Mass. Miss. Mag.,* Preface to vol. ii, 1804; *Panoplist,* July, 1805, p. 77.
(87)   *Mass. Miss. Mag.,* June, 1805.
(88)   *Panoplist,* May, 1807.

Morse sought to unite the Hopkinsian missionary magazine with it. Aided by Leonard Woods, who was regarded as a moderate Hopkinsian, Morse was enabled in 1808 to see his design carried out. The two journals, *The Panoplist* and *Massachusetts Missionary Magazine,* were thenceforth a joint enterprise known as *The Panoplist and Missionary Magazine.* In 1819 the name was changed to *The Panoplist and Missionary Herald,* and since 1820 it has been styled simply *The Missionary Herald.*

The profits of *The Panoplist* for its first year enabled it to contribute to three benevolent enterprises. $100 was given to the Evangelical Society of Vermont for the purpose of aiding poor students for the ministry. $108 was sent to assist the Hampshire Missionary Society, and $21.35 was given to the Berkshire and Columbia Society. (89)

4. THE RHODE ISLAND MISSIONARY SOCIETY

The influence of Samuel Hopkins of Newport was to a large extent responsible for the formation of the Missionary Society of Rhode Island, May 5, 1801. The object of the enterprise was "to promote the gospel in any part of the State where there may be opportunity for it and to assist Africans in coming to a knowledge of the truth in any way which may consist with our means and advantages." Hopkins was made the first president of the Society, and a doctrinal standard was adopted to which missionary candidates were required to subscribe. All workers must acknowledge belief in: 1. The Trinity; 2. The Atonement; 3. Total Depravity; 4. Perseverance of Saints; 5. Election; 6. Preaching as a means of Salvation; 7. Regeneration before taking of Sacraments; 8. Future Rewards and Punishments. The Society had on hand, May 3, 1804, a fund of over $400 which included an African fund of $168.30 secured by Hopkins at the beginning of the Revolutionary War for the purpose of sending colored missionaries to Africa. (90) No religious journal was published by the Rhode Island Society.

(89) *Panoplist,* June, 1806.
(90) *Conn. Evan. Mag.,* April, 1805.

5. THE NEW HAMPSHIRE MISSIONARY SOCIETY

On September 2, 1801 the New Hampshire Missionary Society was instituted at Hopkinton by some ministers and others interested in the extension of evangelical work among the new settlements. Its avowed purpose was "to unite our exertions for spreading abroad the glad tidings of salvation among the Heathen, in our frontier and infant settlements, who are destitute of the precious privileges which we enjoy." (91) Missionaries were sent by the Society, in 1802, to the northern part of New Hampshire, and in the following year to Northern New York. (92) In 1807 a membership of about 100 and receipts of over $2,000 were reported for the previous three years. The distribution of Bibles, testaments, and tracts was a prominent feature of the work of the missionaries. (93) *The Religious Repository,* a bi-weekly missionary magazine, published at Concord, N. H., was the official journal of the Missionary Society. Like most of the missionary journals of the period all profits were pledged to the support of the local society. *The Religious Repository,* however, was not a success. It appeared from September, 1807 to August, 1809. The material included in it was much the same as that which was appearing in *The Panoplist.*

6. HAMPSHIRE MISSIONARY SOCIETY

The Hampshire Missionary Society formed in 1801 was at the outset composed of "all the Congregational and Presbyterian ministers in the County of Hampshire, [Mass.]; of one delegate from each church of the Presbyterian and Congregational denominations in the county; and of all persons who have subscribed and added to the funds of the society as required by the constitution." (94) The Society aimed "to promote the preaching and propagation of the gospel of Jesus Christ among the

(91)   *Conn. Evan. Mag.,* July, 1804.
(92)   *Piscataqua Evan. Mag.,* July and August, 1806.
(93)   *Panoplist,* June, 1807. *Religious Repository,* Sept., 1807 to Aug., 1809.
(94)   *Assembly's Miss. Mag.,* July, 1805.

inhabitants of the new settlements of the United States and the aboriginal natives of the continent." (95)

Four missionaries were sent soon after the formation of the Society to frontier settlements in New York and Maine. (96) Those who went to New York reported the settlements west of the field of labor rent by fierce religious controversies. In 1806 the Society reported the employment of five missionaries in the two regions. (97)   During the period from 1802 to 1807 annual contributions ranged from $1,300 to over $1,500. (98)   The Charitable Female Association of the County rendered substantial aid to the cause. (99)   Expenses ranged from over $900 to

(95)   *Conn. Evan. Mag.*, February, 1802.

(96)   *Panoplist*, Nov., 1805, p. 272.

(97)   *Panoplist*, Oct., 1806.

(98)   From Aug., 1802, to Aug., 1803, $1,510.38, (*Conn. Evan. Mag.*, Feb., 1804).
From Aug., 1803, to Aug., 1804, $1,403.24, (*Conn. Evan. Mag.*, Dec., 1804).
From Aug., 1804, to Aug., 1805, $1,365.95, (*Pan.*, Nov., 1805, p. 274 and Dec., 1805, p. 315, and *Conn. Evan. Mag.*, Nov., 1805).
From Aug., 1805, to Aug., 1806, $1,303.34, (*Mass. Miss.. Mag.*, Nov., 1805).
From Aug., 1806, to Aug., 1807, $1,544.46, (*Panoplist*, Dec., 1807).
From Aug., 1807, to Aug., 1808, $1,242.81, (*Panoplist*, Oct., 1808, p. 233).

(99)   For the year, 1803-04, the Charitable Female Association was credited with contributions to the amount of $262.22. (*Conn. Evan. Mag.*, Dec. 1804).
For 1804-05, $277.88 (*Pan.*, Dec., 1806, and Dec., 1805, p. 316).
For 1805-06, $289.69, (*Pan.*, Oct., 1806, and *Mass. Miss. Mag.*, Feb., 1807.
For 1806-07, $198.01, (*Pan.*, Dec., 1807).
For 1807-08, $167.96, (*Pan.*, Oct., 1808, p. 233)
The Female Association was established in nineteen parishes in Hampshire County. Another female organization which assisted the Hampshire Missionary Society was the Charitable Female Society of Whitestone, N. Y. In 1805 it collected and sent to the missionary society $110. (*Pan.*, Dec., 1806). The following year it voted to send $130. (*Pan.*, Nov., 1807), but seems to have sent but $119, (*Pan.*, Feb., 1808). For 1807 it gave $140, (*Pan.*, Feb., 1808). Membership in the organization was reported as greatly increased from 1805 to 1808. (*Ibid.*).

over $1,300 annually. (100) The chief items of expense for 1805-1806 were listed as "missionaries, books and education of two Indian youths." (101) The Hampshire Missionary Society had no official magazine, but notices of its activities were regularly printed in *The Connecticut Evangelical Magazine* and *The Panoplist*.

7. Piscataqua Missionary Society

At a meeting of the Piscataqua Association of ministers, November 8, 1803, a committee was appointed to draw up a constitution for the Piscataqua Missionary Society. (102) The work of this society was limited in scope, as a statement of its financial resources made May 1, 1805, clearly indicated. The permanent fund was but $208, and a fund designed for annual expenditures amounted to less than $150. (103) The literary journal of the Society was called *The Piscataqua Evangelical Magazine*. It was published at Portsmouth bi-monthly and was pledged to devote all profits to missions. It appeared from 1805 to 1807 only.

8. Maine Missionary Society

The district of Maine which was a part of the Commonwealth of Massachusetts was regarded as a missionary field by quite a number of the local missionary societies. In 1791 the Society for Propagating the Gospel sent workers there, and the first workers of the Massachusetts Missionary Society were sent to the frontier settlement along the Kennebec River. In 1802

(100) The Hampshire Missionary Society reported disbursements as follows:
For 1802-03, $1,344.20, (*Conn. Evan. Mag.*, Feb., 1804).
For 1803-04, $924.90, (*Conn. Evan. Mag.*, Dec., 1804).
For 1804-05, $963.29, (*Conn. Evan. Mag.*, Nov., 1805; *Pis. Evan. Mag.*, May and June, 1806; *Pan.*, Nov., 1805, p. 274; *Pan.*, Dec., 1805, p. 315).
For 1805-06, $1,142.56, (*Conn. Evan. Mag.*, March, 1807, *Pan.*, Oct. 1, 1806; *Mass. Miss. Mag.*, Feb., 1807).
For 1807-08, $1,273.64, (*Pan.*, Oct., 1808, p. 233).
(101) *Conn. Evan. Mag.*, March, 1807.
(102) *Pisc. Evan, Mag.*, Jan. and Feb., 1805. The Association comprised Hon. David Sewall, Rev. Joseph Buckminster, Rev. Huntington Porter, Benjamin Abbot, and Rev. Jesse Appleton.
(103) *Pisc. Evan. Mag.*, May and June, 1805.

there was organized the Lincoln and Kennebec Tract Society which, five years later, through the vote of its members became the Maine Missionary Society. It was incorporated by the Massachusetts Legislature in 1809. Its stated object was "to extend the knowledge of God, our Saviour, and to send the glorious Gospel to those that are destitute of the public and stated means of religious instruction." Its receipts increased rapidly. Sales of *The Panoplist* helped to augment the income of the Society. (104)

9. VERMONT MISSIONARY SOCIETY

The General Convention of Congregational and Presbyterian ministers of Vermont at a meeting held at Middlebury, September 2, 1807, resolved itself into a missionary society. (105)   Prior to that date the Consociation in the Western districts of the State had engaged in missionary work and had issued an address which read in part:

> The remarkable missionary spirit, which has for years past taken place in many parts of the world, among Christians of almost all denominations, is a matter with which we are acquainted . . . . Some contributions were made last year [1805] to the amount of about $328, the principal part of which has been expended in missionary labours. . . . . We most earnestly entreat the assistance of all, according to their several abilities. Should any be able to cast in only two mites, with faith and prayer, it will doubtless yield a plentiful harvest. (106)

The General Convention before it resolved itself into a missionary society collected over $300 for missionary purposes, of which $200 was expended prior to October 10, 1805. (107) After the Missionary Society was launched funds began to pile up

(104)   George B. Little, History of the Maine Missionary Society. Sermon, Jan. 24, 1857.
(105)   *Vt. Evan. Mag.,* July, 1809.
(106)   *Conn. Evan. Mag.,* May., 1806; *Mass. Miss. Mag.,* Aug., 1806.
(107)   *Conn. Evan. Mag.,* May, 1806.

through excess of annual contributions over expenditures, with the result that by 1810 there was a fund on hand of over $1,300. For the year 1809-1810 the expenditures were less than half the receipts. (108)

The Vermont Religious Tract Society was formed in 1808 as an auxiliary to the Missionary Society for the distribution of literature. The General Tract Agent, W. G. Hooker, was also editor of *The Vermont Evangelical Magazine*, the official journal of the Missionary Society. (109) The magazine was issued quarterly at Middlebury and ran from 1809 to 1815. When the last issue appeared in the latter year all the Congregational missionary magazines had perished except *The Panoplist*.

THE PRESBYTERIAN CHURCH MISSIONARY ORGANIZATION

The stronghold of American Presbyterianism in the eighteenth century was in the middle region along the Atlantic seaboard. The Presbytery of Philadelphia was the first to be formed (1704). The region to the South of the Potomac was regarded as missionary territory, and the organization of churches and the settlement of pastors in the region were quite properly considered missionary work. The Brainerd brothers, David and John, who labored among the Indians in New Jersey and Pennsylvania, were ordained clergymen of the New York Synod, as were also Azariah Horton and Samson Occom, who served as missionaries on Long Island and in Central New York. (110)

Before the institution of the General Assembly in 1789, mis-

(108)   *Vermont Evan. Mag.*, Dec., 1810.
      Receipts to July 18, 1808, were $754.51. (*Vt. Evan. Mag.*, Jan., 1809).
      From 1808 to 1809, $734.60, (*Vt. Evan. Mag.*, Jan., 1810).
      From 1809 to 1810, $980.56, (*Vt. Evan. Mag.*, Dec., 1810).
      Disbursements were as follows:
      To July 18, 1808, $137.00, (*Vt. Evan. Mag.*, Jan., 1809).
      1808 to 1809, $628.62, (*Vt. Evan. Mag.*, Jan., 1810).
      1809 to 1810, $412.50, (*Vt. Evan. Mag.*, Dec., 1810).
(109)   *Vt. Evan. Mag.*, Nov., 1809.
(110)   Ashbel Green, *Presbyterian Missions*, pp. 29, 30.

sions had been supported voluntarily by churches and synods. But with the establishment of the General Assembly, a permanent fund for missionaries was obtained through church contributions. In 1795 and 1796 there was expended $1,226.50 for missionary purposes. In 1799 the Assembly was incorporated by Pennsylvania State charter, and the power of holding property for charitable and pious purposes was secured. In this way the General Assembly became a missionary society. (111) Three years later, however, it was deemed best to separate the missionary organization from that of the General Assembly. Accordingly a standing committee of missions was appointed to act throughout the year, clothed with sufficient power to enable it to supervise this important work adequately. (112)

Nathan Ker and Joshua Hart were the first two missionaries to be employed by the General Assembly. They were sent out in 1789 to the frontier settlements of New York and Pennsylvania for a period of three months. Their duties were to preach and administer the ordinances, to organize churches, and to collect information concerning the religious state of the country. (113)

Many people contributed to the missionary fund of the Presbyterian Church in the hope that an Indian mission would be established. Not until 1803, however, was it possible to secure a properly qualified man for the task. Gideon Blackburn had settled among the Cherokee Indians in Blount County, Tennessee, in 1794, and five years later the Presbytery of Union had considered the foundation of an Indian school but had been unable to raise the necessary money. In 1803 Blackburn presented his plan to the Presbyterian General Assembly which

(111)   Extracts from the Minutes of the General Assembly of the Presbyterian Church for the year 1795; *Mass. Miss. Mag.*, June, 1804, p. 12, *et seq.*; July, 1806; *Assembly's Miss. Mag.*, Feb., 1805.

(112)   Ashbel Green, *Presbyterian Missions*, p. 6.

(113)   Acts and Proceedings of the General Assembly of the Presbyterian Church in the U. S. A., 1790. Extracts from the Minutes of the Gen. Assembly.

forthwith contributed $200 toward the school. Blackburn himself raised $430 in Tennessee, and, in 1804, the Highwassee Indian school was opened, with twenty-one children in attendance. (114)

Blackburn's educational work among the Indians received the attention of President Jefferson, and as a result of the latter's recommendation the U. S. Government contributed $250 in 1803, and $350 in 1804 and 1805. In 1808 a second school was organized through funds secured by Blackburn in the South, in 1806, and in the North, where he spent a year. The Southern tour resulted in the raising of $1,500, and in the North he raised from December, 1806, to December, 1807, $5,410.40. In addition to these amounts, $857.95 was secured for the Highwassee School from the Presbyterian General Assembly, the Federal Government, and a Mr. Grant. (115) Blackburn left the mission in 1810 because of difficulties growing out of his efforts to maintain two schools instead of one, and after that date the General Assembly withdrew its aid. (116)

John Chavis, a free Negro of North Carolina, and a graduate of Princeton College, had charge of Presbyterian Negro missions in Virginia and North Carolina. Prior to his employment by the General Assembly in 1801, he had been supported by the Synod of Virginia. The Synod of the Carolinas maintained a school among the Catawba Indians, while the Synod of Pittsburgh undertook the education of a number of young men from various Indian tribes. (117)

In 1802 the Synod of Pittsburgh resolved itself into a missionary organization known as the Western Missionary Society. Its avowed object was "to carry the Gospel to Indians and in-

---

(114) *Assembly's Miss. Mag.*, Feb., 1805; *Pan.*, June, July, and Dec., 1807, and Feb., 1808. Letter from Gideon Blackburn to Jedidiah Morse.

(115) *Pan.*, March, 1808, and April, 1809.

(116) W. Brown, *History of Propagation of Christianity*, vol. iii, p. 427.

(117) *Pan.*, July, 1805, p. 33; *Assembly's Miss. Mag.*, Feb., 1805; Extracts from the Minutes of the Gen. Assembly, 1805.

terim inhabitants." (118)   Joseph Badger, formerly a missionary of the Connecticut and Massachusetts Societies, was appointed in May, 1806, to settle among the Wyandot Indians at Sandusky, Ohio. Three other persons accompanied him to teach the
Indians agriculture and to give elementary school instruction
to the children. The great object of the enterprise was to civilize the Indians. (119)   The war with Great Britain, which followed, completely disrupted the mission.   In 1815 another enterprise was started in Cornplanter's village on the banks of the
Alleghany river. Like the Sandusky mission, its aim was chiefly
educational.   It was not successful. (120)

In like manner, the Synods of Virginia, Kentucky, and the
Carolinas, acted as missionary societies with separate budgets.
These budgets, however, were supervised by a director who was
responsible to the General Assembly. (121)   In 1806 the Synod
of the Carolinas was supporting two missionaries at Natchez
and one in Northwestern North Carolina. (122)   There was also
established, early in the century, the Western Missionary Society
of New Jersey, which was independent of the General Assembly,
but which contributed to its missionary funds.   It disappeared,
however, amid the growing tendency toward national organization and central denominational control. (123)

Four types of people comprised the objectives for the disinterested benevolence of the Presbyterians: those living on the
far frontiers; people in settled regions where churches had not
been organized; the Negro in the South; and the Indians. (124)

(118)   *N. Y. Miss. Mag.*, Feb., 1803.
(119)   *Pan.*, Oct., 1806; Report to Gen. Assembly at meeting, May,
        1806, by Synods which managed missionary business.
        Pan., Feb., 1809.
(120)   Ashbel Green, *Presbyterian Missions*, pp. 40, 41; W. Brown,
        op. cit., vol. iii, pp. 428, 429.
(121)   *N. Y. Miss. Mag.*, Oct., 1803; *Mass. Miss. Mag.*, June, 1804,
        p. 14; July, 1806.
(122)   *Pan.*, Oct., 1806.
(123)   *N. Y. Miss. Mag.*, 1802, p. 207; Ashbel Green, *Presby. Mis-
        sions*, p. 9.
(124)   *Mass. Miss. Mag.*, June, 1804, p. 14; July, 1806.

The Baptists and the Methodists were more active among the Negroes while the Presbyterians were making heroic efforts to educate and civilize the Indians who were willing to have schools established. In 1809 the General Assembly had in its employ sixteen missionaries among the settlers on the frontier in addition to three engaged in teaching the indians and one black man (Chavis) working among the Negroes in North Carolina. (125) Five years later, fifty-one workers were listed as either whole or part-time missionaries of the General Assembly. (126)

At the annual meeting of the Presbyterian General Assembly in 1804 it was arranged that the standing committee on missions should publish a periodical magazine that would serve to communicate to the people such information as might seem to be interesting and useful about missions and other religious matters and which would, it was hoped, pay a profit into the treasury of the Church. (127) The magazine first appeared in 1805 under the name of *The General Assembly's Missionary Magazine or The Evangelical Intelligencer*. It was published monthly at Philadelphia under the editorship of William A. Farrand. Considerable attention was given to the history of missions, notably those of the Moravians, the London Missionary Society, the Baptist Missionary Society in England, and the various missionary organizations in Scotland. It was discontinued in 1809. (128)

MISSIONS OF THE DUTCH REFORMED CHURCH

The old Synod of the Dutch Reformed Church of the United States which preceded the General Synod formed in 1792, began its missionary work in 1789 by starting the practice of taking annual collections in the churches for the support of workers

(125) *Evan. Intelligencer*, June, 1809; Minutes of the Gen. Assembly of the Presbyterian Ch., May, 1809; John H. Livingston, Appendix to Sermon.
(126) Extracts from the Minutes of the Gen. Assembly of the Presbyterian Church in the U. S. A., 1814.
(127) *Gen. Assembly's Miss. Mag.*, Prospectus to vol. i, 1805.
(128) *Ibid.*, 1805 and 1806; *Evan. Intelligencer*, 1807, 1808, and 1809; John H. Livingston, Appendix to Sermon, *op. cit.*

on frontiers. During the period from 1790 to 1810, ministers were sent to Southern New York, Western Virginia, and Mercer County, Kentucky, to organize churches and to visit destitute regions. The Classis of Albany constituted a standing committee for missions. By 1800 it was supporting six workers in Upper Canada. In that year there were nine classes in the General Synod. Contributions varying from ten pounds to twenty-five pounds annually were made by each classis in addition to the special fund provided by the Albany Society. In 1806 the General Synod took over the management of the Canadian mission. The work was disrupted considerably during the next few years, owing to the war with Great Britain, and was ultimately abandoned. The General Synod in 1816 united its missionary organization with the Synod of the Associate Reformed Church and the General Assembly of the Presbyterian Church to form the United Foreign Missionary Society. Its ministers had from the outset been prominent in the two interdenominational societies in New York State. (129)

BAPTIST MISSIONS

Among the Baptists, as among the Congregationalists, the principle of voluntary association was dominant. Disbelieving in anything which resembled an ecclesiastical hierarchy, the Baptists steadfastly refused to delegate power from church to association. Each individual church was pretty much a law unto itself. Unlike the Congregationalists, the Baptists contended for an absolute separation of Church and State. The propagation of religion, they felt, must not only be controlled but financed solely by those interested in it. This aversion to all coercive measures reduced the associations to mere agencies by which, it was hoped, the churches might more effectively promote their enterprises. A Baptist missionary, then, before the organization of societies, was either a worker sent out by a church or an association, or an evangelist, who itinerated regions destitute of

(129)   Edwin T. Corwin, *A Manual of the Reformed Church in America,* 1628-1878, pp. 65-70; 129-141.

churches with the purpose of saving sinners and of organizing Baptist units. In this way the Baptists had increased from less than 10,000 before the Revolution to over 100,000 by the close of the century. The very existence of the denomination was dependent upon the maintenance of the missionary spirit.

In New England the Baptists formed their own missionary societies, altogether independent of Congregationalist organizations, and in Massachusetts and Maine launched missionary journals. The Massachusetts Baptist Missionary Society held its first meeting in Boston, May 25, 1802. It had its origin in the missionary activities of the Warren Association which had sent workers to the northern part of the country in 1778. Thomas Baldwin of the Second Baptist Church of Boston was its most active promoter. Arrangements were made at the first meeting of the Society to send three missionaries to the frontier. Isaac Case, John Tripp, and Joseph Cornell were accordingly sent to Canada, Maine, New Hampshire, and Northwestern New York. The object of the Society was "to furnish occasional preaching and to promote a knowledge of evangelistic truth in the new settlements within these Northern States, or farther, if circumstances should render it proper." (130) Thus it was from the outset a potential foreign missionary agency. Baldwin and John Williams of New York had, for some time, been maintaining a regular correspondence with William Carey at Serampore, India.

A notable feature of the Baptist missionary organization was its open door policy relative to membership. This was all the more remarkable in view of the Baptist emphasis on "close communion." Anyone could join who was willing to pay at least a dollar a year into the treasury. Of the twelve trustees, four might be non-Baptists. The trustees had the power to appoint and dismiss the missionaries at their discretion, and no doctrinal

(130)   *Mass. Bap. Miss. Mag.*, vol. i, Sept., 1803, p. 6;
        Assembly's Miss. Mag., Jan., 1805;
        American Baptist Magazine, Oct., 1825, p. 318.

or other standard was set up for workers. (131)   In 1808 the Legislature of Massachusetts at the request of the Society, granted it a charter so that it could receive bequests and establish a permanent fund for charitable and religious purposes. (132) Over $900 was paid in during 1810 to defray the expenses of maintaining twelve missionaries. (133)   During the following year, September 1, 1810, to September 1, 1811, the receipts reached the peak, $1,471.75. (134)   Thereupon for the next five years a sum of about $1,000 annually was collected. (135)   By 1813 the total receipts of the Society were about $12,000. Twenty missionaries were employed in 1811 at a salary of five dollars per week. (136)

The year following the organization of the Massachusetts Baptist Missionary Society, its journal made its first appearance. For the first fourteen years (1803-1817) Thomas Baldwin of the Second Baptist Church of Boston was its editor.   Baldwin had won fame as a traveling evangelist before he settled in Boston in 1790.   The quarterly magazine known as *The Massachusetts Baptist Missionary Magazine* enabled the Society to reach a wide circle of Baptist readers scattered from Maine to Georgia and to awaken in them a zeal for missions to the heathen.   Full accounts of the labors of the Baptist missionaries in India, South Africa, and the South Sea Islands were printed regularly, along with news of revivals and the progress of American Indian Missions.   In 1817, the name of the magazine was changed to *The American Baptist Magazine*, and beginning in 1825, it was published monthly. (137)

In 1804 two Baptist missionary societies were launched.

(131)   *Mass. Bap. Miss. Mag.*, Sept., 1803, p. 6. (Constitution of Mass. Bap. Miss. Soc.).

(132)   *Mass. Bap. Miss. Mag.*, Dec., 1808.

(133)   *Mass. Bap. Miss. Mag.*, Sept., 1810, p. 352, and June, 1811.

(134)   *Mass. Bap. Miss. Mag.*, Sept., 1811.

(135)   *Mass. Bap. Miss. Mag.*, Sept., 1812, Sept., 1813, Sept., 1814, Sept., 1815.

(136)   David Benedict, *Hist. of the Bap. Denom. in A.*, vol. ii, p. 440.

(137)   *American Baptist Mag.*, Jan., 1826, and Dec., 1828.

In Maine the Bowdoinham Association since 1799 had been supporting Isaac Case as a missionary. The expansion of the work made it expedient for a division of the association to be made, and in 1804, at the time of the division, a missionary society, formed on similar lines to the one in Massachusetts, was launched. A missionary journal, known as *The Maine Baptist Missionary Register*, appeared in August, 1806, but was discontinued after the publication of the second number in 1808. Missionaries were sent to thinly peopled regions of the province and also to New Brunswick. (138)

The other missionary society of the Baptists to appear in 1804 was launched in Philadelphia. It had for its primary object the establishment of a mission among frontier settlers: "nevertheless, they would extend it to the Aborigines of the country when found convenient." (139) Dr. William Rogers of the University of Pennsylvania was made treasurer of the Society. (140)

At Brothertown, N. Y., a Baptist Church comprised of Indian members was organized in 1798. (141) The establishment of the New York Baptist Missionary Society, May 24, 1806, came about as a result of the inevitable disagreement between Baptists and non-Baptists who constituted the original New York Missionary Society, over methods of administering the ordinance of baptism to the Indian converts of Elkanah Holmes. Holmes was obliged to leave his stations in Western New York because of his Baptist allegiance. He was thereupon employed by the New York and Massachusetts Baptist Missionary Societies to labor in Upper Canada among the white settlers. (142)

Three other workers were in the employ of the New York Baptists in 1810. An auxiliary organization existed under the

(138) H. Burrage, *Hist. of the Baptists in N. E.*, pp. 139, 140.
(139) *Assembly's Miss. Mag.*, Jan., 1805; David Benedict, *Gen. Hist. of the Bap. Denom. in America*, vol. ii, p. 442.
(140) *Mass. Bap. Miss. Mag.*, Feb., 1807, p. 283.
(141) David Benedict, *Hist. Bap. Denom*, vol. ii, pp. 426-428.
(142) *Mass. Bap. Miss. Mag.*, Sept., 1810, pp. 328-332.

name of the Baptist Youths' Assistant Society, formed July 23, 1806. (143) The total receipts of the New York Baptist Missionary Society from its formation until 1813 were in excess of $5,000. (144)

Within the next five years numerous Baptist Missionary Societies were formed. The New York Northern and Woodstock Baptist Missionary Societies were organized in 1807. The Genesee Baptist Missionary Society in 1808, the Connecticut Baptist Missionary Society in 1809, and the New Jersey Baptist Missionary Society in 1811 were among the most important local organizations which arose in response to the newly awakened enthusiasm. (145)

Even more numerous than the missionary societies were the women's mite and cent societies, which flourished during the first decade of the century. Among the Baptists as with the Congregationalists the mite societies served as auxiliaries to the missionary organizations. The Boston Female Society for Missionary Purposes, which started in 1800, was composed of Congregationalists and Baptists. After the formation of the Massachusetts Baptist Missionary Society in 1802 the members of the Female Society contributed to their respective denominations separately. (146) The first strictly Baptist mite society was that of Providence, R. I., begun in 1806. (147) About fifty of these societies were to be found among Congregationalists and Baptists before 1814. (148)

In some few instances among the Baptists, missions were carried on, not through the organization of voluntary missionary societies, but through associations acting in a missionary capacity. In such cases, missions to pioneer settlements were merely

(143)   *Ibid.;* Merriam, *Hist. of Amer. Bap. Missions,* p. 8.
(144)   David Benedict, *op. cit.,* vol. ii, p. 442.
(145)   A. L. Vail, *Morning Hour of Am. Bap. Missions,* pp. 116-124; A. H. Newman, *Hist. of Bap. Churches in U. S.,* p. 283.
(146)   *Mass. Bap. Miss. Mag.,* Sept., 1811.
(147)   First Annual Report of the Bap. Board of For. Miss.
(148)   A. L. Vail, *op. cit.,* p. 137.

a continuation of the old established policy of Baptists for extending their work. In Charleston, S. C., a mission was started in 1803 among the Catawba Indians supported by the Baptist Association. In 1807 John Rooker was laboring among the Catawbas with a view to establishing a school for them. (149) During the next ten years, the mission experienced various vicissitudes and was finally abandoned. (150) The Wadmalaw and Edisto Female Mite Society in South Carolina was organized on the same plan as the other mite societies, which gave their contributions to missions, only it made its contributions to the Charleston Association to aid the Catawba Mission. (151)

FRIENDS MISSIONS

The attitude of the Society of Friends toward the aborigines of North America has become proverbial. Quaker apostles to the Indians during the seventeenth century bore witness to the "Inner Light" doctrine of the sect at the time when Eliot and the earlier Mayhews were interpreting the Puritan tenets to their dusky wards in New England. George Fox and William Penn were zealous in their efforts to interpret the Christian message of good will to the red men. John Woolman, likewise, in the following century, at the behest of the Friends General Spring Meeting of 1763, journeyed through the forest to the North branch of the Susquehanna to preach to the Delawares at Wyalusing. Although David Zeisberger had already reached the same place as missionary of the United Brethren, Woolman was cordially invited to deliver his message. Together they labored for three days but as the Indians had already promised Zeisberger that they would become Moravians, Woolman's visit had no tangible result. (152)

(149) *Mass. Bap. Miss. Mag.*, Feb., 1807, p. 283.
(150) A. L. Vail, *op. cit.*, pp.186-189.
(151) D. Benedict, *op. cit.*, vol. ii, p. 442.
(152) John Woolman, *Journal*, pp. 76-96; 163-181; *Aborigines' Committee Pub.*, no. 9, pp. 11-94; Rayner W. Kelsey, *Friends and the Indians*, 1655-1917, pp. 20-32.

The rapid development of the back country following the break up of Pontiac's conspiracy led to the retirement of the Indians of Pennsylvania to a region farther west. Zebulon Heston and John Parrish made a journey to the home of the Delawares in 1773, whose farthest settlements were then 450 miles from Philadelphia. In 1791 Cornplanter, chief of the Seneca nation, visited Philadelphia on government business. He left with the Friends a request that a school be established among his tribe and that two Seneca boys be taken in charge by the Friends and educated. The following year representatives from the Cherokees, Creeks, Chickasaws, and Chocktaws made similar requests. The outbreak of war between the United States and the Indians in Ohio in 1792 gave the Friends opportunity to act as intermediaries in an effort to secure a treaty which would end hostilities and at the same time do justice to the natives. The Philadelphia Yearly Meeting of that year appointed a committee to act. The Treaty Councils of Sandusky (1793) and Canandaigua (1794) were attended by Friends upon the solicitation of the Indians. With the dawn of peace in 1795 the Friends were moved to respond to the urgent appeal of tribal chieftains for schoolmasters and mechanics to teach the Indians. (153)

The missionary labors of the Friends among the Indians began in 1795 when the Philadelphia Yearly Meeting appointed a standing committee of twenty-nine members to direct educational work among the Six Nations in Southwestern New York. The Oneidas were the first to receive the attention of the missionaries sent by the Friends in 1796. The following year several Quakers reached Cornplanter's village on the Allegheny River just south of the New York State line. In 1804 the mission station was moved farther up the river to a place named Tunesassa. This was the most important mission station of the Friends. (154)

Other yearly meetings, in the meantime, were emulating

(153)   *Aborigines' Comm. Pub.*, no. 9, pp. 94-113.
(154)   *Ibid.*, pp. 115-139.

the missionary zeal of the Friends of Philadelphia. The Baltimore Yearly Meeting in 1795 appointed an Indian Committee but made no settlement among the aborigines until 1804. Visits were made, however, during that interval to various tribes in Ohio, and tools were furnished to the Delawares on the Muskingum River. The principal interest of the Baltimore Quakers was centered on the Shawnee Indians. These Indians were located on the Wabash River and came under the spell of the Prophet and his brother Tecumseh. The battle of Tippecanoe followed by the War of 1812 resulted in the destruction of the Quaker Mission in Indiana. After 1815 the Friends of Baltimore directed their efforts toward aiding the Shawnees of Ohio. (155)

The Friends Yearly Meeting of New York began its Indian missionary labors in 1807 when John Dean was delegated to live among the Indians at Brothertown, near Oneida, N. Y. Other Indian tribes in that region received the attention of the New York Quakers, particularly the Oneidas and the Onondagas. After 1820 the emigration of the Indians from that region led to the break-up of missionary work. (156)

Like the other missionary organizations the Friends established schools for Indian children. Every effort was made to emphasize the value of civilized ways in contrast to savage modes of living. Saw mills and grist mills were set up, instruction was given in the use of tools, housekeeping arts were taught the women, and prizes were offered the men for crops raised. The Aboriginal Agricultural Society was formed in 1825 by Joseph Elkinton to further promote this type of Indian education. (157)

(155)   R. Kelsey, *Friends and the Indians,* 1655-1917, pp. 132-142; *Mass. Miss. Mag.,* Oct., Nov., and Dec., 1807. Account of the Proceedings of the Committee appointed for the Improvement and Civilization of Indian Natives by the Yearly Meeting of Friends, held at Baltimore, November, 1805.

(156)   R. Kelsey, *op. cit.,* pp. 114-117.

(157)   *Ibid.,* pp. 89-118; *Mass. Miss. Mag., op. cit.*

CHAPTER IV

THE CRUSADE AGAINST THE ENEMIES OF THE GOSPEL

The excesses of some of the promoters of Jacobinism in France during the course of the French Revolution alarmed most of the conservative clergymen in England and the United States and led them to believe that there was a vast conspiracy of atheists, deists, and liberals of other varieties who were hoping to overthrow the Christian religion and to substitute for it the worship of the Goddess of Reason. To many a timid soul the situation seemed well-nigh hopeless. Only a miracle could save Christendom from complete disruption. To the adventurous and aggressive, however, the boldness of the enemies of the gospel stood as a challenge to take the offensive in a world-wide crusade against infidelity. The immediate objectives of the crusade were the conversion of the Jews and their restoration to Palestine in accordance with Scripture prophecy, the salvation of the heathen, and the confounding of infidelity through the concrete presentation of the truth of Bible prophecy so abundantly fulfilled.

In his *Enquiry into the obligations of Christians to use means for the conversion of the heathens,* published in 1792, William Carey gave new courage to those missionary propagandists, both in Great Britain and the United States, who were anxious to begin such a crusade. He said:

The face of most Christian countries presents a most dreadful scene of ignorance, hypocrisy, and profligacy. Various baneful and pernicious errors appear to gain ground, in almost every part of Christendom; the truths of the gospel, and even the gospel itself,

are attacked, and every method that the enemy can invent is employed to undermine the kingdom of our Lord Jesus Christ.......
All these things are loud calls to Christians and especially to ministers, to exert themselves to the utmost in their several spheres of action, and to try to enlarge them as much as possible. (1)

Four years later Alexander McWhorter in an address before the newly formed New York Missionary Society struck a similar note. After appealing for the support of missions on the customary grounds, he added:

Besides these considerations which address our sense of gratitude and of interest, there is another no less powerful, which arises from the peculiar circumstances of the times. Infidelity abounds. It hath assumed an imperious air, and glories in the expectation of a speedy extermination of the religion of Jesus. To confound its vain hopes, we are called upon to show, by our activity in the cause of truth, that the Spirit of Christ continues to animate His body; that there is still life and energy in His church, and that the prospect is as distant as ever of the gates of hell prevailing against her....... While other parts of the church are earnest and active, let us not be like a palsied limb in a living body. In order to second the efforts abroad, by strenuous efforts at home, let us with cordial affection and mutual confidence, unite our supplications, our counsels, and our resources. Should we even fail in our immediate expectations, we may aid those who shall have better success. And if sinners are brought to the Saviour our object is gained. In the temple above it will make no difference whether they were gathered from the banks of the Mississippi, the Gambia, or the Ganges. (2)

(1) William Carey, *An Enquiry into the obligations of Christians to use means for the conversion of the heathens*, p. 66.

(2) *United States Christian Magazine*, vol. iii, p. 225. The same quotation may also be found in *The Theological Magazine*, June, July, and Aug., 1798, p. 267. For much the same treatment of the relation of missions to the warfare against infidelity see "A discourse delivered in the Chapel of Yale College on Lord's Day, Nov., 23, 1794," by James Dana, pastor of the First Congregational Church of New Haven.

On the other hand, a very pessimistic attitude was taken by the authors of the pastoral letter of the Presbyterian General Assembly in 1798. It was felt that the convulsions in Europe were threatening the very foundation of religion and morality. America, which then seemed to be on the verge of entering the European war, was endangered. Apostasy, impiety, infidelity, and outright atheism, were rampant, it was said. Profligacy and the corruption of public morals seemed proportionate to the decline of religious faith. The last Thursday of August was set apart by the Assembly as a day to be spent by all good Presbyterians in solemn humiliation, fasting, and prayer. (3)

To President Timothy Dwight of Yale College it was evident that infidelity had never in the history of Christendom been more impudently brazen, either in thought or deed, than it had become since the Jacobins began to raise their heads in France. In a sermon preached in New Haven, July 4, 1798, he described in most vivid language some of the orgies which he said had resulted from the general acceptance of Jacobinism there. Some of the frightful effects were to be seen in the more recent tendencies of literary journalism in England. "If I mistake not," said Dwight, "all the Reviews of England, the British Critic excepted, are direct supporters of Jacobinism and Socinianism. Four of them are certainly of this character. Of course, their political and religious opinions will have little weight with the great body of the people of this country." (4)

Well was it for the people of the United States, the pious must have reflected, that they had in men like Dwight and the indefatigable Jedidiah Morse, veritable watchmen of Zion, who would warn them of any danger threatening from abroad. For a most insidious foe called Illuminatism was said to be abroad in the land. In a sermon delivered at Charlestown, April 25, 1799, Morse made the definite charge that Illuminati with secret in-

(3)   *Theological Magazine,* Mch., Apr., and May, 1798, pp. 229-232.
(4)   Timothy Dwight, Sermon, July 4, 1798.

tentions of overthrowing all established governments and relig-
ions were to be found in the United States and that Masonic
lodges in some places contained members committed to the ne-
farious plans of the secret anarchist society. (5) It mattered
little that Morse's charge was later found to be based upon some
vague statements in two European books and that the Illuminati
Society which had originated in Bavaria had long since ceased
to exist. (6) New England Federalists had a decided "will to
believe." Trembling for the old social order became a virtue,
the exercise of which enabled the political and religious conser-
vatives of Connecticut and Massachusetts to regard the Alien
and Sedition Acts as pillars of a sacred temple.

The distress of the pious was nowhere more graphically
portrayed than in an address adopted by the Convention of Massachusetts clergymen (Congregational) at their annual meeting in
1799. The decay of Christian morals was deplored. The prevalence of a spirit of speculation was recognized as a bad sign.
There was said to be a growing disbelief and contempt for the
gospel, a tendency which was being nourished by a spirit of
levity, licentiousness, and pride. The indifference of Christians
was evident in their neglect of the Bible and the doctrines of
the Church, the profanation of the Sabbath, and failure to attend public worship with regularity. Christians seemed to be
merely imitating the world instead of setting an example for
non-Christians. Children were not being instructed in true religious principles. People generally were no longer willing to
trust in Providence but were continually resorting to human
devices to extricate themselves from the consequences of a deplorable national apostasy. What was clearly needed was a revival of primitive Christianity. (7)

---

(5) Jedidiah Morse, Sermon, April 25, 1799. See also Dwight's
     sermon as in note 4.
(6) Vernon Stauffer, New England and the Bavarian Illuminati,
     passim.
(7) *Panoplist,* Feb., 1809.

Not all the orthodox, however, were led to despair. There were those who believed that the time had at last come for Christians to abandon defensive tactics. Especially true was it of the advocates of missions that they refused to concede defeat. In a letter to *The Theological Magazine* in 1798, a contributor who styled himself a "well-wisher to missions" contended that the Church, instead of suffering from outward attacks, was really getting stronger because of her foes. He maintained that the ranks at home would be solidified and the churches strengthened if Christians generally would launch out upon a serious effort to convert the heathen. The moral effect of advancing the outposts would be incalculable. Even if no great number of conversions attended the effort, it would be abundantly worth while to cheer up those who were inclined to despair. (8)

The boldness of British Christians in launching their missionary enterprises at a time when the very foundations of their faith seemed to be trembling appealed to the adventurous. John H. Livingston, in a sermon before the New York Missionary Society in 1799, pictured the situation in that light:

Under the frown of infidelity, and in defiance of that infernal power which, with accumulated energy and fury, is making havoc of the churches, the spirit of the Lord is poured out upon them as waters upon the dry ground, and they unite with a cordiality and come forward with a zeal before unknown. In the Indies, in the islands of the Pacific Ocean, and in Africa, the precious name of Jesus is now proclaimed by their heralds. (9)

The New York Missionary Magazine which appeared in 1800 noted among the signs of the times, "on the one hand, the universal prevalence of error, infidelity, and profaneness. . . . . on the other, the plans which have been recently set on foot, both in Europe and America, for spreading the gospel, and which

(8)   *Theological Magazine,* Jan. and Feb., 1798.
(9)   John H. Livingston, Sermon, April 23, 1799, p. 46.

have received such universal support." (10) The new spirit
of optimism was likewise to be seen in the address to the public,
that same year, of the Northern Missionary Society in the State
of New York. Among other things the report contended: "Though
infidelity and error have burst all usual restraints, and threaten,
like a flood, an universal inundation; yet it may certainly be expected that the spirit of the Lord will raise up a standard to
arrest their progress." (11)

The editors of *The Connecticut Evangelical Magazine* were
from the moment of the first appearance of their journal keenly
aware of the new optimism which was characteristic of missionary promoters. "The abounding corruption of the present age
in sentiment and practice," they said,

and the united efforts of those who hate pure Christianity,
have been seen by the King of Zion, and he appears, in many ways

(10)   *N. Y. Miss. Mag.*, vol. i, 1800, pp. 1-3.
(11)   *N. Y. Miss. Mag.*, 1800, p. 105.   The idea of missions as a
       "standard" to be erected against infidelity was also expressed in an
       article in the *Conn. Evan. Mag.*, Nov., 1802, which told of the
       activities of the Berkshire and Columbia Missionary Society. The
       article went on to say: "The work which is thus begun is a great
       and good work. It has taken place, as we conceive, in conse-
       quence of the late effusion of the Holy Spirit, both in Europe
       and America. And, while God's spirit is poured out, it is hoped
       that a standard will be supported against the enemies of Christ's
       kingdom."
           The Christian's Magazine designed to promote the knowledge
       and influence of evangelical truth and order appeared in 1806. Its
       avowed design was "to throw something into the common scale."
       The editor further believed that "this work will fulfill its task
       by erecting a standard around which the friends of truth may
       rally." (*Christian's Magazine*, 1806, p. xi).
           In an address to "Christians of every denomination" the Lower
       Piscataqua Association of Ministers at the time of the launching
       of the Piscataqua Missionary Society said: "Violent exertions are
       making on the side of irreligion. Many are they who avowedly
       combine against the Lord, and against His anointed. They con-
       centrate their strength with determined perseverance. Ought men
       to sleep while the enemy is sowing tares? Shall the children of
       the world forever be wiser than the children of light? . . . .
       We derive great encouragement, in our present attempt from a
       consideration of the extraordinary exertions to the same pur-
       pose," [i. e. missions]. (*Conn. Evan. Mag.*, April, 1804).

to be raising a standard against his enemies while they attempt to come in like a flood. He hath arisen and come forth from his place, and is bathing the sword of his justice in the blood of those who have most openly denied him, or idolatrously departed from the purity of his gospel. (12)

The minutes of the Presbyterian General Assembly for 1802 voiced the new confidence by saying:

The influence of that vain philosophy which has spread its infection through many of our cities, and even insinuated itself into the remote parts of our country, corrupting society, and poisoning the very principles of moral action, has been greatly diminished. Infidelity, which a few years since threatened, by its artful seductions, to undermine the foundations of virtue, and by its open assaults, to break down the barriers of religion, is now seldom heard of, in many of the congregations within our bounds. (13)

Three years later a committee of the same denomination appointed to investigate and report on the state of religion in the United States confidently asserted that, "the pernicious and destructive principles of infidelity and philosophy, falsely so called, continue to lose their influence or are less avowed." (14)

An article signed "Observator," which appeared in *The Panoplist* in 1807, summarized the reasons why all the faithful should rejoice. The foundation of the African institution in England, the abolition of the slave trade by act of Congress, and the extensive missionary work on the frontier and in the wilderness were among the favorable signs of the times. Secret, combined, and formidable attempts to crush the Christian religion had merely resulted in greater exertions on the part of those loyal to the gospel, pure and undefiled. As a direct outcome of

(12)   *Conn. Evan. Mag.* Introduction to July, 1800.
(13)   *N. Y. Miss. Mag.* Minutes of the Gen. Assembly of the Presby. Ch., 1802.
(14)   *Panoplist,* July, 1805, p. 34.

these increased efforts to defend the faith, the gospel was being preached in the Pacific, in South America, Africa, in the islands of the Indian Ocean, in India, China, and Tartary, in Northern Europe and North America. In a short time the gospel would literally be preached to every creature under heaven. Learned men were translating the Scriptures into the languages of heathen nations. Bibles were being distributed in a wholesale manner. The Jews were being reached by the gospel. Truly it was a day of God's power. (15)

As the crusade against the enemies of the gospel became more aggressive its leaders succeeded in enlisting the support of many of the Old Calvinists who had hitherto been lacking in enthusiasm because of their distrust of the Hopkinsians. Toward the obligations of the Great Commission which called for the evangelization of the world, the Old or Moderate Calvinists had displayed a remarkable indifference. But the assault of the Edwardean or Hopkinsian wing upon every variety of liberalism tended to draw all Calvinists together in the common enterprise.

In order to make the victory of righteousness more complete, the self-appointed defenders of the faith sought to link up every species of liberalism with the worst horrors of the reign of terror and the worship of the Goddess of Reason. New England liberalism might by a considerable stretch of the imagination be pictured as resembling deism, much as American republicanism might be shown to have traits in common with Jacobinian democracy. All that was needed was that the two insidious foes, infidelity and liberalism, be exposed as differing only in degree, but actually constituting two similar phases of a dangerous movement which threatened the overthrow of the old social order. Morse and Dwight, far from desiring to shirk their duty in this respect, entered with buoyant enthusiasm and zeal upon the task of purifying the Congregational churches of New England. Soon all Congregationalism was astir with the noise of battle.

The two most prominent liberal tendencies within New

(15)   *Panoplist,* Dec., 1807.

England Congregationalism were Universalism and Arianism, or Unitarianism, as the latter was coming to be styled. There was, it is true, at the beginning of the nineteenth century, only one avowedly Unitarian church in Boston where the liberal element was entrenched. King's Chapel which had been Episcopalian before the Revolution became a Unitarian church in 1785 under the leadership of its pastor, James Freeman. (16)   In 1791 Clark Brown of Brimfield, Mass., was refused installation by a church council because of his Arian views. (17)   But the movement, for the most part, was centered in Boston.   The presence of Timothy Dwight, "the pope of Connecticut" and "the last of the Puritans," at the head of Yale College was sufficient guarantee to the keepers of truth and orthodoxy that liberal heresy would never make headway in New Haven.   It was found necessary, however, at a meeting of the General Assembly of Connecticut at Weathersby, June 17, 1806, to grapple with the enemy within the Church and to give him no more quarter than would have been accorded a deist or a skeptic. The committee's report, as accepted, read:

Whereas a few individuals in the ministry have openly denied the divinity and personality of our Lord and Saviour Jesus Christ, Voted, That this Association, feeling it a duty to bear testimony against principles so subversive of the pillars of gospel truth, of vital piety and morality, do recommend to their brethren in the State, earnestly to contend for the faith once delivered to the saints; and to hold no communion, and to form no exchange in ministerial duties with preachers of this character. (18)

Yale College had been the training camp for such vigorous orthodox preachers as Jonathan Edwards, Samuel Hopkins, Stephen West, John Smalley, Nathaniel Emmons, and Timothy

---

(16)   Joseph H. Allen, *An Historical Sketch of the Unitarian Movement since the Reformation,* pp. 186, 187.

(17)   Williston Walker, *Ten New England Leaders,* p. 387.

(18)   *Panoplist,* November, 1806.

Dwight. All these men were natives of Connecticut, all were New Calvinists of the revivalistic type, all undertook to train students who were in turn to assume an aggressive leadership in advancing the outposts of Christianity. Their influence was felt not merely in New England but throughout the nation. Edwards himself had gone in his last days to Princeton to become the President of the Presbyterian College there. His son and namesake was President of Union College in Schenectady during the last two years of his life. So influential did the aggressive Edwardean revivalists become that there was soon no middle ground possible between the liberalism of the Boston Unitarians and the dogmatism of the New Calvinists. Forced to make a choice, the Old Calvinists, for the most part, cast in their lot with the revivalists because of their adherence to orthodox tenets, rather than with the cultured liberals with whom the moderates were in closer sympathy emotionally. The task of bringing together the two orthodox wings was greatly expedited through the labors of Leonard Woods and Jedidiah Morse.

It remained for a clear-cut issue to arise between Calvinism and liberalism to achieve the ends desired by Morse and his colleagues. That issue was furnished in the election of a successor to Dr. David Tappan of Harvard College, whose death in 1803 left vacant the Hollis Professorship of Divinity in that institution. The power of appointing the members of the college faculty was vested in the College Corporation of six members, but their action was subject to the approval of the Board of Overseers which was made up of the members of the State Senate and the whole body of the Congregational clergy of Boston and vicinity. (19) At first the vote in the Corporation was a tie between the orthodox candidate, Jesse Appleton and the liberal, Henry Ware. In February, 1805, the deadlock was broken and Ware was elected. The election was ratified by the Board of Overseers by a vote of thirty-three to twenty-three.

(19)   William B. Sprague, *The Life of Jedidiah Morse*, p. 58.

Morse, who naturally opposed Ware's election, along with Senator Titcomb and Abiel Holmes, had made an unsuccessful effort to prevent the ratification of the choice. Failing in his design he published a pamphlet of twenty-eight pages, entitled "The True Reasons on which the election of a Hollis Professor of Divinity was opposed at the Board of Overseers, etc." (20) The publication of this pamphlet marked the beginning of a protracted war which resulted in the rending of Congregationalism in twain.

The Monthly Anthology which had been launched in 1803 as a liberal literary journal took sharp issue with Morse's pamphlet and a vigorous controversy ensued. The election of an anti-trinitarian to the Divinity chair was nothing less than a challenge to the orthodox party to consolidate their ranks and drive the liberals out of the Congregational Church. That fact that Thomas Hollis who had established the professorship in question had expressly provided that no theological test should be required of candidates for the position in no way daunted the champions of orthodoxy. (21) The church must be purified of her insidious enemies. The day of compromises was past. To Morse there was urgent need for a medium of propaganda which would be more effective than pamphlet publication. If the enemy was to be assaulted effectively it was necessary that he be assaulted sys-

(20)   Ibid., p. 63. Harvard College, Morse maintained, had been founded by men who were orthodox and should be kept from deviating from the standards and beliefs of its founders. The motto on the college seal was " Christo et Ecclesiae." Hollis, the founder of the Divinity chair, had believed in the doctrine of the Trinity and in the total depravity of man. The successful candidate in the February election had doubtful opinions concerning these two pillars of Calvinism. Morse believed he was contending for an eternal principle, the abandonment of which was certain to be the prelude to disaster. Taking for his text, as it were, the college motto, he dilated somewhat at length, concluding in an ecstatic, if not poetic mood, "For Christ and the Church was the ancient college founded by men we delight to call our fathers; for Christ and the Church has it hitherto been cherished, instructed, and governed by men of like Christian principles and spirit; for Christ and the Church, oh may the God of our fathers, who still lives and reigns, in mercy preserve it, so long as the sun and moon shall endure."

(21)   Josiah Quincy, History of Harvard University, vol. ii, p. 285.

tematically and regularly rather than sporadically. It was with a view to providing such an organ of attack that Morse inaugurated a new religious journal which he fittingly styled *The Panoplist*. His plan for the publication of the magazine was cordially approved by Timothy Dwight and several other Hopkinsians, but it was not at first heartily welcomed by the Massachusetts Hopkinsians who had already launched *The Massachusetts Missionary Magazine*. Nathaniel Emmons and Samuel Spring were two of the most prominent Hopkinsians who had to be won over in order to secure the desired unity of action in the impending struggle. Through the skillful diplomacy of Leonard Woods and Morse, the Hopkinsians were induced in 1808 to unite their missionary organ with *The Panoplist*. The Reformed Confessions adopted by the Puritans seemed to the leaders who were promoting the cause of Calvinist harmony to be the best basis for doctrinal unity. (22)

It was the chief aim of *The Panoplist* to arouse the slumbering forces of orthodoxy, no matter what might be the minor doctrinal peculiarities which had seemed important hitherto, and to assail all the insidious foes of the faith once delivered to John Calvin. There was another important service, however, which *The Panoplist* sought to render. Morse and the other promoters of the new magazine were ardent missionary enthusiasts. Subscribers to *The Panoplist* were kept informed of the work of the English missionaries in Asia, Africa, and the islands of the Pacific. The work of the missionaries of several New England societies was given publicity. In 1809 Jeremiah Evarts of New Haven was induced to accept the editorship of *The Panoplist and Missionary Magazine*. (23) Material from *The London Evangelical Magazine* and *The London Christian Observer*, both missionary organs, was freely utilized in order to awaken American Christians to a sense of responsibility toward missionary enterprises. Full accounts appeared telling of efforts being

(22)   Leonard Woods, *History of Andover*, p. 41.
(23)   William B. Sprague, *Life of Jedidiah Morse*, p. 67.

made by tract and Bible societies to distribute religious
literature, of the activities of the women's mite societies, and
of the rise and progress of benevolent organizations of various
kinds. Thus the warfare of the orthodox Calvinists against liberalism in New England aided the missionary cause in providing
a means of publicity for missions on a much larger scale and in
a much more effective manner than had been possible through
the magazines sponsored by the missionary organizations themselves. The crusade itself attracted attention and helped to link
up the missionary enterprise with something of unusual importance at home.

Another enterprise which was destined to be of benefit to
the development of the missionary spirit in the country was the
establishment of the Divinity School at Andover, Mass. After
the election of Ware to the Hollis professorship at Harvard relations between the college authorities and the orthodox religious
leaders of Massachusetts ceased to be cordial. Eliphalet Pearson, a Calvinist professor, resigned shortly after Ware's election,
and Morse conceived the idea of securing his services for a new
theological seminary which it was hoped might soon be founded.
The constitution of Phillips Academy at Andover seemed to provide a solution of the difficulty. The Academy had been founded in 1778 by two brothers, Samuel Phillips of Andover and John
Phillips of Exeter. In 1789 the latter had given $20,000 to the
institution for the "virtuous and pious education of youths of
genius and serious dispositions." In his will he left one-third
of his estate for charitable scholars and ministerial students.
William Phillips of Boston had given $4,000 for the same pur-
pose. In addition to this gift he left at his death a legacy of
$15,000 for the Academy and $10,000 for a theological institution. The chief object of the Academy as stated in its constitution was the promotion of true piety and virtue. (24) It seemed to Morse and his advisers that in Andover was to be found
the solution of the problem of the Divinity School.

(24)   Abiel Abbot, *History of Andover*, p. 115.

An obstacle which had to be removed, however, before the new project could be successfully launched was the hostile attitude of some of the Hopkinsians, especially Nathaniel Emmons of Franklin and Samuel Spring of Newburyport. These two clergymen had been contemplating a theological seminary of their own to be set up at Newbury, Mass., and had so far advanced their project that they hesitated to give it up. They had induced three wealthy men to finance the proposed institution. The backers were William Bartlett and Moses Brown of Newburyport and John Norris of Salem. It required the utmost strategy on the part of Morse and Woods to persuade the Hopkinsians to give up their seminary and their missionary journal and to unite in both enterprises with the other Calvinists. The Hopkinsians were finally conciliated through the promise that they would be given adequate consideration in the management of the Divinity College. (25)

The trustees of Phillips Academy secured from the Massachusetts legislature in 1807 the right to receive and hold donations for a theological institution. The widow and son of Lieutenant-Governor Phillips erected two buildings. Samuel Abbot of Andover gave $20,000 as an endowment for the establishment of a Professorship of Theology and for the support of students. Later he left as a legacy to the institution $100,000. The three who had agreed to promote the proposed Hopkinsian seminary at Newbury were likewise induced to support the Andover project. Moses Brown donated $10,000 and William Bartlett $30,-000. John Norris of Salem, a merchant, who had for some years engaged in the East India trade, according to a story later current in New England, donated $10,000 in silver which he had previously packed away in firkins with the intention of keeping the money until an American foreign missionary project should be launched. Norris was led to believe that the missionary cause

(25)   Leonard Woods, *History of Andover,* p. 69.

would be advanced through the establishment of the Divinity School. (26)

In stressing the importance of the proposed new seminary *The Panoplist* contended that it would serve to eliminate the differences which had hitherto tended to keep the forces of orthodoxy divided, while at the same time it would aid to promoting the rift which had already begun to appear between Unitarians and Calvinists. (27)   After the opening of the school the hopes of *The Panoplist* were increased. No longer would the church suffer from the evil of an uneducated ministry.

We are deliberately of the opinion [said the editor] that the Seminary is not only by far the most important institution that ever was in the United States; but also that the annals of the Christian Church furnish no instance of a theological school, which at so early a stage of its progress, could boast of such a matured and extensive plan; such ample funds; and such brilliant prospects both of honor and usefulness.

Especially happy was the editor to realize that the Old Calvinists and the Hopkinsinians had united their funds and their organs of propaganda in the common enterprise.

We are glad [said he] to find that they have waived smaller points of difference, and to make a common cause against the grievous and destructive errors, which infect our churches. When multitudes around us are denying that Jesus is the Christ, and destroying the hopes of the soul; ought not those who concur in all the fundamentals of the truth as it is in Jesus to lose sight of minor differences among themselves, and to take the field together against the common enemy? (28)

(26)   Abiel Abbot, *History of Andover*, pp. 119, 120. For the story about Norris and the silver dollars, see, A. E. Dunning, *Congregationalists in America*, p. 288.

(27)   *Panoplist*, Dec., 1807, pp. 314, 315.

(28)   *Panoplist*, Jan., 1809. See also *Panoplist*, Feb., 1809, p. 416, for a reply to a criticism of the Divinity School, which had been made by *The Monthly Anthology*.

Two professors and thirty-six students constituted the personnel of the new seminary during its first year (1808-1809). Leonard Woods was installed as Abbot Professor of Christian Theology, and Eliphalet Pearson became Professor of Sacred Literature. Pearson, however, resigned after serving a year, because of his dissatisfaction with the Hopkinsians whom he considered altogether too influential in the management of the Seminary. In 1810 his place was filled by the appointment of Moses Stuart. Dr. Edward Griffin who accepted the Bartlett Professorship of Pulpit Eloquence in 1809 resigned two years later to become pastor of the Park Street Church in Boston, the new citadel of orthodoxy in the enemy's territory. (29) Despite considerable friction between the two Calvinistic parties at Andover the institution experienced a steady and substantial growth.

Among the thirty-six students who were present at the opening of the Divinity College in October, 1808, were Adoniram Judson and Gordon Hall, both destined to sail to India within four years as missionaries to the heathen world. Among the new recruits in 1809 were Samuel J. Mills and James Richards, the latter to win distinction for heroic services as missionary to Ceylon, the former to be immortalized for his intense devotion to the whole missionary cause both at home and abroad. Of these four men all but Judson had been educated at Williams College. Mills and Richards with three other students at Williams had met and prayed in 1806 that the gospel might be sent to the heathen in Asia. Fired by the enthusiasm of Mills, the young men had organized what was called the Society of the Brethren. Strict secrecy was adopted as a guiding principle in the proceedings of the Brethren. The five original signers of the constitution were Ezra Fisk, Luther Rice and John Seward, together with Mills and Richards. The constitution and the records of the society were brought to Andover in 1809 when Mills and Richards entered. (30)

(29)   Abiel Abbot, *History of Andover,* pp. 120-123.
(30)   J. H. Hewitt, *Williams College and Foreign Missions,* pp. 46, 75.

Membership in the Society of the Brethren was not restricted to those who were pledged to become foreign missionaries, but included others who were sufficiently interested to make the cause a subject of inquiry. (31) Still Mills felt that the utmost care should be exercised in admitting candidates. Two clauses in the constitution made clear the purpose and the constituency of the society:

"The object of the Society shall be to effect in the person of its members, a mission or missions to the heathen.

"No person shall be admitted who is under any engagement of any kind, which shall be incompatible with going on a mission to the heathen." (32)

The constitution was written in cipher in view of the need of securing absolute secrecy. From Andover, Mills wrote to Richards, March 20, 1810:

Let us be more cautious in the admission of members than ever the Illuminati. We shall do well to examine their every look, their every action, above all see that they are possessed of ardent piety. Let them take hold, as it were, of the angel of the covenant. Let their souls go out to God in fervent supplication that the heathen might be given to Jesus Christ for an inheritance. (33)

Among the new members admitted at Andover, after a close investigation as to their qualifications were Judson, Nott, and Newell, all among the first to sail for India as representatives of the American Board of Commissioners for Foreign Missions. (34)

Societies similar to Mills' Society of the Brethren were organized in other colleges. Middlebury College which had been

---

(31) *Memoir of American Missionaries,* p. 14. At Williams College the original society seems to have been limited to prospective missionaries.

(32) J. H. Hewitt, *op. cit.,* p. 42.

(33) *Ibid.,* p. 75

(34) *Ibid.,* p. 46.

founded in 1800, partly as a result of the religious revival which swept Vermont, had attracted quite a number of students who were interested in the extension of the Christian frontier. These students organized a Brethren's Society after learning about the Williams College Brethren. In 1814 some students at Princeton likewise patterned a Society after that of Mills. Attempts to start Brethren societies at Union and Dartmouth failed. At Andover the beginnings of a missionary library were made. (35) Missionary propaganda was published by the Society, notably the Memoirs of Claudius Buchanan and David Bogue's answer to those who were raising objections to missions. Both these publications were of English authorship and appeared in their first American editions in 1811.

(35)   *Memoir of American Missionaries,* pp. 14, 20-21.

CHAPTER V

FROM WEST TO EAST

During the last quarter of the eighteenth century considerable information was being published about many lands and peoples, hitherto almost unknown. The books which told of the three voyages of Captain Cook to the islands of the Pacific aroused the wonder and curiosity of the reading public in England and America. Men like Carey and Kicherer in perusing the pages of these books of exploration and adventure thought about the deplorable religious condition of the pagans that Captain Cook had encountered. (1) James Bruce having journeyed through Abyssinia discovered the source of the Blue Nile. (2) Mungo Park, a Scotch adventurer and medical practitioner, penetrated fifteen hundred miles into the very heart of the Dark Continent. (3) Truly was the prophecy of Daniel being fulfilled, which read: "Many shall run to and fro, and knowledge shall be increased."

American periodical literature was giving considerable attention before the close of the century to various customs and ideas of heathen peoples. It was true that descriptions of such peoples were accounts which had first appeared in British publications, but this fact in no respect lessened their importance to the American reader. In 1792 a Philadelphia journal, destined like so many others of the period to have a brief existence, which was styled *The Lady's Magazine and Repository of Enter-*

(1)   *Conn. Evan. Mag.,* Oct., 1804.
(2)   David Jenks, *A Study of World Evangelisation,* p. 109.
(3)   *Theological Magazine,* Sept., Oct., and Nov., 1798; For an account of the death of Mungo Park see *Panoplist,* July, 1806.

taining Intelligence, was edifying its readers with glowing accounts of strange lands and peoples. Among its geographical and anthropological lore might be found: "Curious Accounts of the Inhabitants of the Empire of Japan, their Government, Manners, and Customs"; "A Concise Account of the Empire of Hindustan"; "A Visit to the Infant Teshoo Lama"; and "The Customs and Manners of Different Nations," among which were to be found lands inhabited by Turks, Persians, Arabians, and Hindus. (4)

Another short-lived Philadelphia magazine, *The Monthly Review,* made its appearance in 1795. It was devoted entirely to a review of books. Among current publications discussed were: Buchanan's *Travels in the Western Hebrides from 1782 to 1790; Asiatic Researches,* a part of which was written by Sir William Jones, the distinguished Orientalist; *Travels among the Kalmuks and Tatars;* and Niebuhr's *Travels through Arabia and other Countries in the East.* (5) *The American Moral and Sentimental Magazine,* published in New York for a few months in 1797 and 1798, undertook to instruct its readers through narratives of remarkable occurrences and strange vicissitudes which travelers were experiencing in various parts of the world. (6) As many as sixty-three new ventures in the world of periodical literature were made during the decade from 1790 to 1800. (7) While most of them were ephemeral they none the less served to direct the attention and stimulate the interest of people along new lines of knowledge, especially with reference to the rapidly accumulating store of information concerning the world and its inhabitants.

The Theological Magazine, published in New York from 1795 to 1799, was the first American journal to give publicity to the work of the English missionaries in India and in Otaheite

(4)   *Lady's Magazine,* June, July, Aug., Oct., and Nov., 1792.
(5)   *American Monthly Review,* vol. i, 1795.
(6)   *American Moral and Sentimental Magazine,* July 3, July, 17, July 31, Aug., 14, Aug. 28, Sept. 11, Sept. 25, Oct. 9, Oct. 23. Nov. 6, Nov. 20, and Dec. 4, 1797.
(7)   William Beer, *Check List of Periodicals,* 1741-1800, p. 4.

(Tahiti). In it articles from English and Scotch missionary magazines, including letters from the missionaries to friends at home, were reprinted. Accounts of the work of Carey and the Anglican chaplain, John Clark, in Sierra Leone, originally published by *The Edinburgh Missionary Magazine,* were made available for American readers in the pages of *The Theological Magazine.* (8) Religious enterprises were linked up with deeds of daring and stories of adventure. The perilous journey of Watt and Winterbottom from Sierra Leone to the Foulah country in the interior of Africa was described with fulsome praise for the heroic missionaries. (9) The sentiments of Baron von Schirnding of Saxony on the desirability of attempting to evangelize the whole heathen world were likewise made known to American readers. (10) With the rise of the missionary journal proper, as the official organ of the local missionary society, the public was educated on the subject of foreign missionary enterprises with ever increasing effectiveness. It was the period of world politics, and serious people were thinking in terms of humanity as never before. For the British missionaries to go to India, Africa and the South Seas at a time when people were directing their attention to geography and anthropology, however crude their notions may have been, meant that missionary enterprises would be certain to receive a degree of attention hitherto impossible. What the missionary magazines in America accomplished was not simply the stimulation of popular curiosity but, as a more significant result, the enlargement of the conception of duty on the part of American Christians.

Direct contacts between people in America and some of the British missionaries during the first decade of the nineteenth century opened up a new channel of communication between West and East. Dr. William Staughton of Philadelphia, an Englishman by birth and education, was present at Kettering in 1792 on the occasion of the formation of the Particular Baptist

(8)   *Theological Magazine,* June and July, 1797.
(9)   *Ibid.*
(10) *Theo. Mag.,* Mch. and Apr., 1797.

Missionary Society. The following year he came to America and, after laboring for a dozen years in South Carolina and New Jersey, became pastor of the First Baptist Church of Philadelphia. (11) Staughton was an ardent advocate of the East Indian missionary enterprise and wrote a book about it. The chief purpose of the book, apart from its educational purpose, was to collect money for the British missionaries. (12)

Robert Ralston was another Philadelphian who was interested in the Serampore mission. Ralston was an East India merchant and an elder in the Second Presbyterian Church of which Dr. Ashbel Green was pastor. He was an intimate friend of Captain Benjamin Wickes who had carried some Baptist missionaries from England to India in 1799. In 1805 Wickes forwarded one thousand guineas to Ralston for safe ,keeping until he should make his next voyage. The money had been entrusted to Wickes by the directors of the Baptist Missionary Society for the aid of Carey who was engaged in translating the Bible into several languages of the Hindus. Upon his arrival in Philadelphia, Wickes made the suggestion that Americans be invited to add to the sum collected in England. A circular letter from the ministers of Philadelphia to the clergy of other cities gave hearty endorsement to the plan suggested by Wickes. The leading missionary journals gave the appeal the widest possible publicity. The circular calling for aid for "the benighted idolaters of one-eighth of the human race" was signed by Staughton and White, the Baptist pastors; by the rector of St. Paul's, Episcopalian; the pastor of St. George's, Methodist; by four Presbyterian ministers and several others. Committees were appointed to receive funds in New York, Boston, Portsmouth, New Haven, Newark, New Brunswick, Baltimore, Washington, Alexandria, Norfolk, Charleston, and Savannah. (13) Between five and six thousand

(11) A. L. Vail, *The Morning Hour of American Baptist Missions*, pp. 327-331.

(12) W. Staughton, *The Baptist Mission in India.*

(13) *Pan.*, Mch., 1806, pp. 462-464; *Conn. Evan. Mag.*, Apr., 1806, and Jan., 1807; *Assembly's Miss. Mag.*, April and October, 1807.

dollars was raised at the time, although most of it was secured in Philadelphia and Boston. (14)   Carey and his colleagues sent a letter addressed to the Christian congregations in the United States, without regard to denominational affiliations, thanking them for their generosity and telling them of his hopes for further translations of the Bible. (15)   His letter was published in several missionary magazines.

The work of the London Missionary Society was likewise given publicity in America through the republication of British magazine material.   Especially noteworthy were the articles which were appearing in *The Panoplist* telling of the labors of the missionaries who had sailed to the island of Otaheite on the ship Duff in 1796-1797, and of the work being undertaken by Kicherer and Vanderkemp in South Africa.   An account of the visit of two converted Hottentots to London (16), a letter from King Pomare of Otaheite, praising the missionaries for the help they had rendered his subjects in teaching them a better way of living, (17) descriptions of the customs of the "Boschemen" of South Africa, a wild race said by the missionary Kicherer to have had no idea of a Supreme Being and no form of worship, except admiration for a certain insect, (18) all these items and many others of like import were appearing regularly to keep

(14)   *Conn. Evan. Mag.*, Jan., 1807, p. 271; *Assembly's Miss. Mag.*, Oct., 1806, pp. 493, 494.
        Andrew Fuller, the Secretary of the English Baptist Missionary Society, in a letter to a friend in Philadelphia, dated June 3, 1806, said: "We make an annual collection in London. I have several times made it, but never till this spring collected more than four hundred pounds.   This time the collection amounted to upward of eight hundred pounds. Of all the nations upon earth, I think it is the great duty of Britain and North America to disseminate the gospel. We have more commerce with mankind, more gospel knowledge, more liberty, more wealth, than perhaps any other nations; and while we are thus employed, or rather while there is amongst us a body of Christians thus employed, I have little or no apprehension of our falling a prey to the destroyer." (*Assembly's Missionary Magazine*, Oct., 1806, p. 494).

(15)   *Pan.*, Apr., 1807.

(16)   *Pan.*, July, 1808; *Conn. Evan. Mag.*, Oct., 1804.

(17)   *Pan.*, Sept., 1808.

(18)   *Pan.*, July, 1805, p. 30, *et seq.*

alive the interest of Americans in the work of the interdenominational missionary society of London.

The program of world evangelization was calling for an extension of the field in the East. The decision of the London Society to send Robert Morrison to China had a direct influence in advancing the missionary interest of Americans. Missionaries of the Society frequently made the voyage to the East by way of America. Early in 1807 Morrison arrived in New York with two other workers of the London Society who were bound for India. The party was welcomed by John M. Mason, pastor of the Associate Reformed Church and a prominent figure in the New York Missionary Society. After a brief stay in New York the missionaries proceeded to Philadelphia to be received by Robert Ralston and Ashbel Green. Among the prominent Americans interested in missions who met the English recruits while they were in the United States were Captain Wickes, Gideon Blackburn, missionary to the Cherokee Indians, John H. Livingston, pastor of the Dutch Reformed Church of New York, John McKnight, one of the United Presbyterian pastors of New York, and William Rogers of the University of Pennsylvania, a prominent Baptist of Philadelphia. Ralston secured from Secretary of State Madison a letter recommending Morrison's design to the American consul at Canton and asking the consul to render the missionary all the assistance he could, consistent with the interests of the United States. After Morrison reached China further aid was extended him through a friend of Ralston, a Mr. Milnor, at a time when the outcome of the Chinese mission seemed decidedly uncertain. It is quite probable that the mission would have failed completely but for American aid and encouragement. Morrison had only the happiest memories of his relations with Americans. (19)

The existence of the British colony of Sierra Leone, made up as it was of a number of free Negroes from Nova Scotia and

(19)   E. A. Morrison, *Memoirs of the Life and Labors of Robert Morrison,* pp. 106-157.

about two hundred white people who had gone there before 1794, (20) was a powerful aid to missionary propaganda in the United States because it linked up the free Negro question with the program of missions. David Grigg and James Rodway were sent there by the English Baptist Missionary Society in 1795 to labor among the Negroes. (21) The following year the Edinburgh Missionary Society sent Peter Ferguson and Robert Graham to aid in the cause. Their report giving in detail some of the more intimate features of their daily life, with the Scotch emphasis on the importance of teaching the natives thrift and economy, must have struck a responsive chord in its American readers, especially in those from New England. Speaking of the missionaries, the report said:

They take along with them a variety of mechanical instruments, and implements of agriculture. The plan of introducing the useful arts in connection with the gospel in heathen countries, appears to us pregnant with the most essential advantages. It not only tends to meliorate the condition of the natives, to call into action their dormant faculties, which are strengthened and improved in proportion as they are exerted, as well as to bring them into a position more favorable for attending to religious instruction, thus fulfilling the direct end of the Missionary Societies; but it is also a system of prudence and economy, highly requisite to be pursued as a means of preserving the pecuniary affairs of such institutions from the possibility of embarrassment. . . . . . . (22)

The population of the colony in 1811 was about 2,000, and by 1814 it had increased to about 3,000. There were a number of schools there and six places of worship at the latter date. (23) In 1815 thirty-eight free Negroes left Boston for Sierra Leone

(20)   S. J. Mills, *A View of Exertions Lately Made*, etc., pp. 21-23.
(21)   *U. S. Christian Magazine*, 1796, no. 2, p. 147; W. Staughton, *The Baptist Mission in India*, p. 26.
(22)   *Theological Magazine*, Oct., Nov., and Dec., 1797, p. 83.
(23)   S. J. Mills, *op. cit.*

under Paul Cuffee, a half-breed from the Elizabeth Islands off the coast of Massachusetts, who had previously been in the employ of the New York Missionary Society. (24)

The earliest foreign mission field to be contemplated by Americans was Africa. It was the interest that Samuel Hopkins of Newport took in the unfortunate slave population of the United States that led him to devise a plan which contained both missionary and colonization features. His idea was formulated in a circular issued under the joint signature of himself and Ezra Stiles. Stiles was then (1776) pastor of the Second Congregational Church of Newport, and while in most matters he differed quite sharply with his friend Hopkins of the First Church, yet to the plan of sending black missionaries to Africa he and Hopkins were able to agree. Accordingly, Bristol Yama and John Quamine, two young Negroes, went to Princeton to study theology under Dr. Witherspoon in order to fit themselves to be native evangelists to their pagan brethren across the Atlantic. The Hopkins-Stiles circular received the approval of the associated ministers of several counties of Connecticut and of the New York Presbytery. Thirty pounds was given to the African fund by the Scotch S. P. C. K., and over fifty pounds was raised in New England. (25) The interruption of the pastoral work of Hopkins at Newport, due to the British occupation of the city, and other difficulties growing out of the war made the African project impossible of execution. In 1791 Hopkins sought to renew the plan and to send Bristol Yama and Salmur Nubia to Africa, but when he died in 1803 his missionary hopes were still unfulfilled. His plan in 1791 was to have the abolition societies which were then being formed in various parts of the country act as missionary agencies. (26)

Samuel J. Mills, Jr., was twenty years old when Hopkins

(24)   W. B. Sprague, *Life of Jedidiah Morse*, p. 128, *et seq.*
(25)   Samuel Hopkins, *Works*, vol. i, pp. 129-134. Memoir by Park.
(26)   *Ibid.*, pp. 119-166; A. Alexander, *History of Colonization on the West Coast of Africa*, p. 58.

died. His father, a Congregational minister of Torringford, Conn., was an admirer of Hopkins and a believer in his peculiar theology. Young Mills was interested in Hopkins's African plan and seems to have had an African mission in mind before turning his attention to the Asiatic field and promoting the interest which led to the formation of the American Board of Commissioners for Foreign Missions. Mills died at sea in 1818 while engaged in work for the African Colonization Society. (27) He had been instrumental in promoting the organization of the Foreign Mission School at Cornwall, Conn., where a number of young men from various islands of the Pacific (including the youth Obookiah from Hawaii whom Mills found in New Haven in 1810 and sent to Andover), from Asiatic countries, and from several American Indian tribes were brought together to be trained as missionaries to their respective peoples. This plan was similar to the one advocated by Hopkins, in that it involved the training of natives for missionary work. (28)

The American Board of Commissioners which at the outset sponsored the Foreign Mission School at Cornwall was an agency designed by New England Congregationalism to carry the gospel to the heathen across the sea. Its organization was inevitable in view of the practical break-down of American Indian missions, the increasing tendency of churches in newly settled areas to support themselves, the general prosperity of the nation, and the ardent desire of Christians in America to emulate their British brethren in the work of evangelizing the world. Increasing knowledge of the larger world as revealed by travelers and explorers, direct contacts with British missionaries enroute to the East, and the educational work of the local missionary magazines—all these factors made their contribution toward the ultimate organization of national missionary societies which would carry the banner of Christianity to the heath-

(27)   Hopkins, *Works,* vol. i, p. 164.
(28)   *Pan.,* July, 1810; Sept., 1810; Sept., 1811; July, 1816; Feb., 1817; Nov., 1817; *Religious Tract Society Publications,* Second Series. (London, 1820) ; G. Spring, *Memoir of S. J. Mills,* p. 10.

en outside the borders of the land. In giving financial assistance to William Carey for the purpose of aiding him in his translation enterprise, American Congregationalists, Baptists, and Presbyterians experienced a sense of satisfaction in the realization that they were engaging in the larger work. Eastern missions, then, were the product of a number of forces, all working quietly beneath the surface of American Christianity.

The immediate cause of the organization of the American Board was the ardent desire of four young men who were students at Andover to engage in missionary work somewhere in the East. Adoniram Judson, Samuel J. Mills, Samuel Nott, and Samuel Newell presented a paper to the General Association which met in 1810 at Bradford, Mass., advocating a foreign mission and expressing their willingness to serve as missionaries. The General Association turned the business over to a committee of three clergymen who reported in favor of forming the American Board of Commissioners for Foreign Missions. Among the nine members of the Board as it was originally constituted were the Governor of Connecticut, President Dwight of Yale College, Samuel Spring and William Bartlett of Newburyport, and Samuel Worcester of Salem. Jedidiah Morse of Charlestown was elected to membership the following year. (29)

The original plan of the Board was to have nine members, five of whom were to be elected by the General Association of Massachusetts and four by the General Association of Connecticut. This arrangement was carried out for one year only, however, as in 1811 the Board was incorporated by the Massachusetts legislature with power to elect its own members. In 1813 thirteen new members were chosen, distributed as follows: two from New Hampshire, one from Vermont, one from Massachusetts, one from Rhode Island, four from New York, and two from New Jersey. Prominent Presbyterians among the new members elected in 1812 were Ashbel Green, President of the College of

(29)   Joseph Tracy, *History of the American Board*, pp. 447-450; W. B. Sprague, *Life of Jedidiah Morse*, p. 162.

New Jersey, and Robert Ralston of Philadelphia. The Pruden-
tial Committee transmitted annual reports to the General Associations of Congregational ministers of New Hampshire, Massachusetts, and Connecticut to the General Convention of Congregational and Presbyterian ministers of Vermont, and to the
General Assembly of the Presbyterian Church. (30)

John Norris of Salem, who had been one of the outstanding
financiaı supporters of Andover Theological Seminary, died late
in 1808 leaving his estate to his widow who died in 1811. (31)
Mrs. Norris left a legacy of $30,000 to the American Board which,
however, was not immediately available because of litigation
on the part of some relatives. (32)   Donations to the Board
came in rapidly as a consequence of the enthusiasm of its promoters and the liberality of a few wealthy benefactors. Between
the annual meeting of September, 1811, and June 20, 1812, over
$12,000 was collected, $7,000 of which came from four donors
and about $4,000 from various auxiliary societies. (33)   The
remarkable success of the new enterprise enabled its members
to consider the feasibility of sending a few missionaries to the
East.

In the meantime the Board, not anticipating such a rapid
augmentation of resources, had sent Judson to England to inter-
view the directors of the London Missionary Society for the purpose of arranging some sort of joint responsibility for a new
Oriental mission.   After experiencing capture and imprisonment
at the hands of the French, Judson reached England and was
cordially received by the Directors, but was told that too many
difficulties were involved in the proposal of the American Board.
They were willing to receive the four young men as their own
agents, but firmly declined to share with their American brethren

(30)   *Panoplist*, Oct., 1812; *Memorial Volume of the First Fifty Years,*
        etc., pp. 405-407; Tracy, *History of the American Board*, pp.
        447-450.
(31)   Hopkins, *Works*, vol. i, p. 56; *Panoplist*, Mch., 1811.
(32)   *Panoplist*, Oct., 1812.
(33)   *Ibid.*

the responsibility of directing the proposed mission. Upon Judson's return to America the material resources of the Board were in so much better shape than had been expected that it was decided to send Judson, Newell, Nott, and their wives, together with Luther Rice and Gordon Hall to India. It was not certain at the outset just where in the Far East a mission would be most advantageously located, but the concensus of opinion seemed to be that the Burman Empire offered the most favorable opportunity, as Burma was not in the British Empire and was not receiving the attention of the British missionaries. (34)

Early in 1812 the missionary party sailed, but not all on the same ship. Judson and Newell with their wives set out from Salem for Calcutta, while Nott and his wife, Rice, and Hall sailed from Philadelphia. On the ship with the latter were several British missionaries of the London and English Baptist societies. (35) In the course of the long voyage to India Judson and his wife experienced a change in their belief concerning the proper way of administering baptism and, upon their arrival, were received as members of the Baptist Church at Serampore, after being immersed by Ward, a colleague of William Carey. Judson thereupon severed his connections with the American Board. A few weeks later Rice followed suit for the same reason. Newell went to Ceylon after the death of his wife and child. Hall and Nott proceeded to Bombay after having been ordered to leave Calcutta by officials of the British East India Company who professed to regard them as American spies. After considerable difficulty with these officials the missionaries were permitted to stay in Bombay. (36)

The Bombay mission begun by Hall and Nott was reinforced by the arrival of Newell who came from Ceylon early in 1815. Arrangements were thereupon made for a mission in Northern Ceylon, which was started in 1816 by James Richards and three

(34)   *Panoplist*, Sept., 1811, and Oct., 1812.
(35)   *Pan.*, Oct., 1812.
(36)   *Pan.*, Aug., 1813, Nov., 1814, Dec., 1814.

other young men who had shortly before been ordained at Newburyport. (37) The Bombay and Ceylon missions were the only ones undertaken by the American Board prior to 1820.

The withdrawal of the support of the Presbyterian General Assembly from Blackburn's Cherokee Indian mission in 1810 and the suspension of the Wyandot Mission of the Western Missionary Society (Synod of Pittsburgh) due to the outbreak of the War of 1812 marked the close of an era in Presbyterian missions among the aborigines. Unsuccessful efforts were made to establish a mission in Cornplanter's town on the Allegheny and another among the Indians located near Lewistown, Ohio. A new era began, however, with the establishment of the United Foreign Mission Society in 1817, which aimed to "spread the gospel among the Indians of North America, the inhabitants of Mexico and South America, and in other portions of the heathen and anti-Christian world." Its constitution was ratified by the General Assembly of the Presbyterian Church and the General Synods of the Reformed Dutch and Associated Reformed Churches. Hon. Stephen Van Rensselaer was the first president of the Society. (38)   Its first mission among the Indians was not begun, however, until 1820. (39)

The change of sentiments on the part of Judson and Rice proved to be most significant in the history of the Baptist denomination. *The Massachusetts Baptist Missionary Magazine,* edited by Thomas Baldwin of the Second Baptist Church of Boston, from its origin in 1803 had laid special stress on the worldwide aspect of missions. The translations of the Scripture, directed as they were by the Baptist Carey, and the assistance which had been rendered to Carey through the Ralston-Wickes appeal had made the Baptists of America aware of the important place their denomination was already assuming as a missionary agen-

(37)   *Pan.,* Feb., 1815, Apr., 1815, July, 1815, Jan., 1816, Oct., 1817, and Jan., 1818.
(38)   *Pan.,* Sept., 1817.
(39)   Ashbel Green, *Hist. of Presby. Missions,* pp. 40, 41.

cy. In 1812 the Salem Bible Translation and Foreign Mission Society was formed with Lucius Bolles, the Baptist minister of Salem, as president. Its object was "to raise money to aid the translation of the Scriptures into the Eastern languages, at present going on at Serampore under the superintendence of Doctor William Carey; or, if deemed advisable at any time to assist in sending a missionary or missionaries from this country to India." (40)   Early the following year word reached America of the resignation of Judson and Rice from the American Board's staff in India, due to their change of views. To Baldwin of Boston the news seemed providential.   Under his leadership there was organized without further delay the Baptist Society for Propagating the Gospel in India and other Foreign Parts. (41) Nearly $1,000 was raised by the new society before the close of the year 1813. (42)

A letter from Rice to Baldwin, dated Bahia, Brazil, June 5, 1813, told of Rice's intention of visiting the United States to solicit aid for the establishment and maintenance of a Baptist Mission in India. As to suggestions for methods, Rice felt that Baldwin and the other missionary promoters in America could arrange details better than one who had been away from the country for over a year. His own attitude was less uncertain as was clear from his concluding statement:

Impelled by the strong tide of my anxious feelings, I should proceed to use entreaties relative to the formation of a Baptist Missionary Society, or the adoption of some measures by the Baptist Churches in America, for the effectual and permanent patronage offered to them by so remarkable a dispensation of divine Providence. (43)

Meanwhile, Mr. and Mrs. Judson were encountering diffi-

(40)   *Mass. Bap. Miss. Mag.*, Sept., 1812.
(41)   *Ibid.*, Mch., 1813.
(42)   *Ibid.*, Dec., 1813.
(43)   *Mass. Bap. Miss. Mag.*, Sept., 1813.

culties in their relations with the hostile East India Company. Fearing transportation to England they left Madras where they had been staying with some British missionaries and proceeded to Rangoon, Burma. Shortly after his conversion to the Baptist fold Judson had written to Baldwin: "Should there be formed a Baptist Society for the support of a mission in these parts, I shall be ready to consider myself their missionary." (44) The news of the plight of Judson reached America about the same time that Rice arrived and the conjunction of events made it imperative that the Baptists should act without further delay. The General Missionary Convention of the Baptist Denomination in the United States of America for Foreign Missions was the result.

Luther Rice was eminently qualified for the immediate task at hand. At the time of his arrival from India in September, 1813, there existed no effective bond of unity among the 2,000 and more Baptist churches in the country, except such as was afforded through the medium of the voluntary regional associations. No systematic effort had been made, other than an unsuccessful attempt of Morgan Edwards prior to the Revolution, to coordinate the associations. Baptists were inherently suspicious of all centralizing tendencies as dangerous to their dearly acquired liberties. It was the task of the Baptist leaders who favored the foreign missionary cause to construct an organization, or at least provide an agency, which would have adequate powers to deal with the business entrusted to it and still not encroach upon the liberties of the churches. It seemed wise to have Rice tour the South before any plan for a national missionary organization should be made. In October, 1813, largely as a result of Rice's efforts, an organization similar to the one formed at Boston earlier in the year was made in Richmond, Va. In December the Philadelphia Baptist Society for Foreign Missions was formed. (45) A circular address issued December 17, 1813 by the Savannah Baptist Society for Foreign Missions called on the in-

(44)   Edw. Judson, *Life of Adoniram Judson*, p. 43.
(45)   *Mass. Bap. Mag.*, Dec., 1813, pp. 353, 354; Mch., 1814.

habitants of Georgia and the adjacent parts of South Carolina "to embrace the present auspicious moment, and engage with joyful haste and determined energy in the great work of evangelizing the poor heathen." (46)   In February, 1814 a Baptist Missionary Society was formed in New York. Baltimore, Fredericksburg, and Washington likewise witnessed the formation of similar societies before the meeting of the national convention on May 18. (47)

Philadelphia was the place agreed upon as the most advantageous meeting-place for the convention. Thirty-three delegates represented the Baptists from all parts of the United States. Missionary societies and churches constituted the basis of representation. Thomas Baldwin of Boston was elected president of the permanent board established to transact missionary business. Among prominent Baptists who attended the Philadelphia Convention were Richard Furman of Charleston, S. C., Henry Holcomb, William Rogers, William Staughton, and William White of Philadelphia, Lucius Bolles of Salem, John Williams of New York, and Stephen Gano of Providence, R. I. Among honorary members chosen were the Philadelphia Presbyterians, Captain Wickes and Robert Ralston. Luther Rice was employed to continue his itinerant services. Judson was accepted as missionary of the Board, and arrangements were made for his support. It was agreed that the General Convention should meet once in three years. Delegates from missionary societies and other religious bodies of the Baptist denomination which should contribute at least one hundred dollars annually were to comprise the Convention. Twenty-one commissioners made up the Baptist Board of Foreign Missions. An address was drawn up and sent to the churches and to all interested in religion, calling attention to the need of the hour and to the opportunity offered through the organization of the Convention. (48)

(46)   *Ibid.,* Mch., 1814.
(47)   First Annual Report of the Bap. Bd. F. M.
(48)   *Mass. Bap. Miss. Mag.,* Sept., 1814.

The formation of auxiliary societies to assist in financing the new enterprise was greatly facilitated by the exertions of Rice during the year following the Philadelphia Convention. The Connecticut Society Auxiliary to the Baptist Board of Foreign Missions formed at Hartford, August 31, 1814, was the first of a number that were called into being. The Union Society in Vermont and New Hampshire, the Vermont Society, the Dublin, N. H., Society, the Evangelical Society of Bristol and Newport Counties, R. I., the Union Society of Plymouth County and Vicinity (Mass.), the Utica, N. Y., Society, and the Sansom St. [Philadelphia] Baptist Female Society for Promoting Foreign Missions were all formed before the close of 1814. (49)   There were by that time in existence twenty-two Baptist missionary societies in the United States, counting the local societies formed during the first decade of the century. (50)

According to a report made by Rice to Dr. Staughton in 1815 practically all the Baptist associations, 115 in number, were favorable to the foreign missionary enterprise. Even in the South where he had rather expected to encounter opposition, favorable responses had been the rule. Some associations had not responded at all, but Rice attributed their failure to reply, in most cases, either to carelessness or indifference rather than to anti-mission sentiment. From June 20, 1814 to May 10, 1815 the Board received from all sources $1,059.15. (51)   During 1816 over $6,000 was reported. (52)   From April to August, 1817 the total receipts were well over $11,000. (53)

Previous to the year 1819 when the Missionary Society of the Methodist Episcopal Church was formed there was no line of demarcation between missions and evangelism. The labors of Bishop Asbury and the Methodist preachers under his direction were intended to bring about the expansion of the Wesleyan

(49)   *Ibid.*, Mch., 1815; First Annual Rep. of Bap. Bd. F. M.

(50)   *Mass. Bap. Miss. Mag.*, Mch., 1815.

(51)   First Annual Report of the Bap. Bd. F. M.

(52)   *Mass. Bap. Miss. Mag.*, June, Sept., and Dec., 1816.

(53)   *Am. Bap. Mag.*, Sept., 1817.

organization wherever people could be found who might consent to organize a class meeting or a Methodist society. Pioneers, Negroes, and Indians, alike, all had souls to save, and therefore were looked upon as proper candidates for membership in Methodist churches, once they had experienced the requisite conversion. Difficulty, however, was experienced in attempting to preach the gospel to the Indians, because of the fact that Methodist preachers were not equipped educationally to grapple with the linguistic problems necessarily involved in conducting an Indian mission. So no regular work was begun before 1820. Asbury had often thought of them and their need of the gospel and as early as 1789 wrote in his diary: "I wrote a letter to Cornplanter, chief of the Seneca nation of Indians. I hope God will shortly visit these outcasts of men, and send messengers to publish the glad tidings of salvation amongst them." (54)

The very year of Asbury's death (1816) John Stewart, a colored man who had experienced a regular, sudden Methodist conversion, began preaching to the Delaware Indians at Goshen, Ohio, and to the Wyandots on the Upper Sandusky. The remarkable results which attended Stewart's evangelistic labors so stirred the Methodist Conference that the organization of a missionary society was felt to be imperative by that body. (55)

As to the foreign missionary project it was believed inexpedient for Methodists to participate until their ranks had been sufficiently consolidated at home. Asbury, writing in 1815 at Washington said:

A Baptist missionary came into town collecting for foreign lands: we labor for those at home. . . . As our Baptist brother talked and read letters upon missions to foreign lands, I thought I might help with a few words. I related that a few years past, a London Methodist member in conversation had complained to me that the kingdom and the church had given so large-

(54) Asbury, *Journal*, vol. ii, p. 52.
(55) J. M. Reid, *Missions and Missionary Society of the M. E. Church*, vol. i, p. 322.

ly to support distant missions. I observed, in reply, that the Methodist preachers, who had been sent by John Wesley to America, came as missionaries: some of them returned but all did not. And now behold the consequences of this mission. (56)

Two other entries in Asbury's Journal make abundantly clear his approval of the foreign missionary projects of others, however unwise he may have felt it would be for Methodists to attempt any of their own. In 1806, commenting on his reading, he said:

I have read Mungo Park's Travels in Africa; certain parts are sc extraordinary, that it appears like a romance. If true, he experienced astonishing hardships. It would seem by this narrative, that the Africans are in a state so wretched, any suffering with the gospel would be submitted to in preference. (57)

Again in 1809 he noted: "I have read with satisfaction the Star in the East: Lord hasten the time when all shall know thee." (58)

Asbury's close relations with Thomas Coke at whose hands he received his ordination and who was regarded as another superintendent of Wesleyanism in America along with Asbury (although Coke was absent much of the time) kept the Methodists in America in close touch with the missionary work of the English Wesleyans. In 1786 the Missionary Society under Coke's leadership began work in the British West Indies. In 1808 Coke was released from his American duties in order to make it possible for him to give all his time to the direction of missions. He was on his way to Ceylon to begin a Wesleyan mission there when he died in 1814. He had crossed the Atlantic eighteen times in connection with his duties in the United States, Nova Scotia, and the West Indies. He had been supported, it is true, by the English Conference, but American Methodists acquiesced in his missionary labors with the consciousness that it would be at the

(56)   Asbury, *Journal,* vol. iii, p. 385, 386.
(57)   *Ibid.,* vol. iii, p. 138.
(58)   *Ibid.,* vol. iii, p. 273.

cost of his services to them. They felt that in this way they would be sharing in the task of world wide evangelism which their English colleagues were promoting. (59)

The time had not come to send Methodist missionaries across the seas from the United States, but a fertile field was inviting them among the Spanish and French inhabitants of the recently acquired possessions west of the Mississippi. (60) Thus American Methodism, always missionary, strove consistently toward the consolidation of enterprises already under way in order to secure rallying centers for an ever widening area. After each consolidation there followed as a matter of course an outreaching toward some new region which was beckoning to its evangelists. New England, Canada, the Middle West, the Southwest, the Indian reservations, the lands beyond the Mississippi, finally the lands across the seas — each in turn witnessed the labors of Methodist missionaries. In 1825 the Methodist Board expressed its willingness to send a missionary to Liberia, but it was not until 1832 that Melville Cox, American Methodism's first foreign missionary, was sent there. (61)

(59)   Samuel Drew, *Life of the Rev. Thomas Coke,* etc.:
        Nathan Bangs, *History of the M. E. Church,* vol. ii, pp. 376-379;
        John Telford, *A Short History of Wesleyan Methodist Foreign Missions,* p. 43.
(60)   J. M. Reid, *Missions and Missionary Society of the M. E. Church,* vol. i, pp. 27, 28.
(61)   *Ibid.,* vol. i, pp. 153-157.

CHAPTER VI

PROPHECY, PRAYER, AND PROPAGANDA

The closing years of the eighteenth century seemed gloomy and forboding enough to serious observers on both sides of the Atlantic. The Reign of Terror and the rise of Bonaparte following the overthrow of the old French Monarchy threatened the foundations of the social order throughout Christendom. Some of the effects of the revolutionary philosophy of Europeans were being sensibly felt by members of the Federalist aristocracy in America, engaged as its protagonists were in' a hopeless effort to stem the rising tide of Jeffersonian republicanism. The popularity of deism was evident in the avidity with which Paine's *Age of Reason* was being received. Wars and rumors of wars, Jacobin intrigues, and the assaults of infidel philosophy were topics sufficiently sensational for the most flamboyant of the orthodox clergymen, while recurrent visits of the yellow fever scourge served as final proof to the defenders of the faith that divine wrath had at last taken notice of the great apostasy in America. Were not all these unusual and fearful happenings the prelude to the millenium, as foreseen by Biblical writers? The signs of the times were highly suggestive that the last days were near.

The unusual turbulence of the closing decade of the century and the newly awakened interest in missions led to a reexamination of prophecy. Conversely, the contributions of preachers and students of prophecy to the interpretation of vague passages in the Bible constituted a not inconsiderable part of the dynamic of missions. It is difficult to see how any effective missionary propaganda could have been developed without an incessant appeal to Bible prophecy as a final authority in regard to the duty of Christians to evangelize the world. By an appeal to prophecy infidelity could be refuted. Prophecies which were being fulfilled in contemporary events constituted a most valuable part of the armory of the believer in his contest with skepticism. Deism and all its fallacies would ultimately pass away when confronted with the unmistakable evidence afforded by the long delayed fulfillment of Scripture. (1)

To John M. Mason, who preached the missionary sermon of 1797 before the New York Missionary Society, the temporary success of the infidel constituted not simply a challenge; it served as an aid to faith because it verified the Scriptures. One of the signs of the approaching end of the age would be a poverty of faith on the earth. "Every infidel under heaven is a witness for Christianity and carries in his forehead the proclamation that it is divine." (2)   Such optimism was not likely to be daunted by any difficulties which the new missionary enterprises might encounter.

Within the politico-ecclesiastical hierarchy of Calvinist Federalism in Connecticut, Timothy Dwight was an outstanding figure. Dubbed by his foes "the Pope of Connecticut," his leadership among New England Congregationalists was unquestioned. At an hour when war between the United States and France was regarded as inevitable the citizens of New Haven requested Dwight to deliver the annual fourth of July sermon. Dwight's analysis of the international turmoil was made in the light of the sixteenth chapter of the book of Revelation. It was clear to the famous President of Yale that the prophetic writers of Scripture had the closing decades of the eighteenth century in mind when they uttered many of their dark sayings. The book of Revelation might be difficult for the masses to understand, but

(1)   Uzal Ogden, *Antidote to Deism; The Deist Unmasked,* vol. i, pp. 186-192; vol. ii, p. 94.

(2)   John M. Mason, Sermon preached in the First Presbyterian Church of New York before the N. Y. Miss. Soc., Nov. 7, 1797, *Hope for the Heathen.* Vol. iii of the works of John M. Mason.

not for Timothy Dwight. The sixth vial of Revelation 16:12 was just about to end. During the period of the pouring out of this vial, the Jesuit order had been suppressed, the Roman Catholic clergy had been shorn of some of their power, the revenues of the Pope curtailed, and the French kingdom overthrown. All of these events the great seer of Patmos had predicted seventeen centuries before. The beast and the false prophet referred to by the sacred writer were to be understood as the papacy and the Catholic clergy. The unclean spirits were the false teachers in Catholic countries, such as the philosophers and the encyclopaedists of France. John had foreseen not merely such general movements as those leading up to and accompanying the French Revolution, but such minutiae as the appropriation of the French Academy by the philosophers and the rise of the Society of the Illuminati whom Dwight characterized as "atheistical, anarchical, communistic, licentious, and Jesuitical." Well might the adversaries of the true church tremble in view of the vindication of prophecies whose fulfillment had been so long delayed. The destruction of papal Babylon might be expected at any moment. The return of Christ to earth would be followed by the glorious day of God's elect. (3)

There was a virtual unanimity among Bible scholars that the forty-two months of Revelation 11:2 and the "time, times, and half a time" of Daniel 12:7 were to be understood as twelve hundred and sixty years. During this interval Antichrist was expected to flourish. By Antichrist most Protestants meant the pope, although some felt that the sultan of Turkey was an Eastern Antichrist. (4) It might be objected by the skeptic that this method of interpretation was questionable and that the prophecies

(3)   Timothy Dwight, The Duty of Americans at the present crisis, illustrated in a discourse preached on the fourth of July, 1798; at the request of the citizens of New Haven.

(4)   William Linn, The Signs of the Times; U. S. Christian Magazine, 1796, p. 142; John H. Livingston, The Glory of the Redeemer, Sermon; Conn. Evan. Mag., July, 1800, p. 7, Sept., 1800, p. 91; George S. Faber, A General and Connected view of the Prophecies, etc.

were obscure. To William Collins who preached the annual sermon before the Baptist Missionary Society in Boston in 1806 such objections seemed trivial. The obscurity of prophecy served a purpose in that it enabled the Church to conceal her designs from her enemies, who, steeped in skepticism, were unable to understand projects, such as the missionary movement, until after they were well under way. The calling of the Gentiles was clearly a subject of prophecy. The spread of the gospel would result in the gradual Christianizing of the earth. The missionary spirit was being manifested everywhere, and the Jews would be converted, in all likelihood, in the near future. Other favorable signs, according to Collins, were the translation of the Bible into various languages of India and the tottering condition of the Roman Catholic Church. (5)

Although the apocalyptic writers had so clearly specified the duration of the antichristian age as 1,260 years, they had, for some providential reason, not indicated the exact date of its beginning. There was some disagreement among the Bible students of the land as to the correct date when Antichrist or the papacy had arisen. In the year 606 A. D., according to many, was to be found an event which seemed to mark the recognition of a pope for the first time. In that year, it was claimed, Pope Boniface III was made the first universal Bishop. The millenium then would begin in 1866. All enemies of Christ would be overthrown before that date, according to Elijah Parish in a sermon delivered before the Congregational Missionary Society of Massachusetts, in 1807. God had poured great wealth upon America. In view of the brevity of the interval remaining for the completion of the task of evangelizing the world everyone ought to contribute. The single cent of the poor would help. (6)

It was not the orthodox only who were led to believe through the perusal of the prophecies that the end of the age was at

---

(5) William Collins, Sermon preached before the Massachusetts Baptist Missionary Society, May 28, 1806.

(6) Elijah Parish, A sermon preached before the Massachusetts Missionary Society at their annual meeting in Boston, May 26, 1807.

hand; Unitarians and Universalists were likewise aware of the signs of the times. There was, for instance, Joseph Priestley whose Unitarianism was so pronounced that many even of the unorthodox of the Massachusetts clergy shunned him, after he came to America, while Calvinists shuddered at his name because of his rejection of their fundamental tenets. Nevertheless, Priestley adhered rigidly to the prevalent vogue of interpretation where vague prophecies were involved. (7) In like manner, Elhanan Winchester, a Baptist-Universalist, whose ideas about the ultimate restoration of the whole human race to a state of millenial bliss were detested by the orthodox of every shade, was an ardent believer in the orthodox ideas about the nearness of the millenium. In a course of lectures which he delivered in Southwark, England, he elaborated his interpretation of "Prophecies that remain to be fulfilled." Calculating by means of a mathematical analysis of a passage in Revelation that the Turkish Empire was destined to wane towards the close of the eighteenth century and within a few years to pass forever, he added; "How vastly important is the period to which we are approaching; and what great things are at the door! Infidelity may laugh, and triumph for a time, but its props will fall away every year, till the whole superstructure shall come down." (8)

Samuel Hopkins, an ardent believer in foreign missions, in his "Treatise on the Millenium" claimed that the popes rose to power in 257 A. D. This discovery served as a remarkable corroboration of the veracity of the Bible, because exactly 1,260 years later Luther began his attack on the Church. 1517 A. D. marked the beginning of the period of papal decline. Assuming that in 606 A. D. the pope arose to the high dignity of a universal ruler, the end of the age would come in 1866. Hopkins further believed that the period of the beginning of the millenium could be determined by a calculation of the number of years that had

---

(7)   Joseph Priestley, *The Present State of Europe compared with the Antient Prophecies.*

(8)   Elhanan Winchester, *A Course of Lectures on Prophecies that remain to be fulfilled,* vol. i, p. 137.

elapsed since creation. As the creation of the world in six days had been followed by a Sabbath of rest, it was not unreasonable to expect that six thousand years of turmoil would be succeeded by the Sabbath of the Church, the millenium. Did not the Scripture say that a thousand years were with God as a day, and a day as a thousand years? Now, according to the best calculations, the six thousand years would terminate before another century had elapsed. Christians were urged by Hopkins to use means for the conversion of the heathen, although some miracle would probably be necessary for the completion of the task. (9)

The rise of Napoleon Bonaparte to power in France during the decade overlapping the centuries furnished new material for missionary propaganda based on a study of prophecy. Napoleon might be the "eighth king" mentioned in Revelation 17:11. Just as confidently as students of prophecy had interpreted the signs of the times during the earlier stages of the French Revolution in the light of every unusual occurrence, forecasting the utter discomfiture of the papacy, they now, upon receipt of the news concerning the Concordat between Napoleon and the Pope, were made aware of the fulfillment of Revelation 13:12 which told of the healing of the wound of the beast. The setting up of Catholic establishments in the Rhenish Confederation, in Holland, and in Switzerland were clear evidences of the truth of Biblical prophecy. The great apostasy of these nations would be the last. The Concordat, said John B. Romeyn of Albany, N. Y., would last fifty years; then the millenium would begin. (10)

Christian ministers were indeed increasingly impressed by the sinister wickedness of Napoleon as he continued his mad career. His rise and fall must surely have been foreshadowed by prophetic writers. A careful study of the Scriptures yielded much comfort to those who were longing for the day of Zion's

(9)   Samuel Hopkins, A Treatise on the Millenium; *Works*, vol. iii, pp. 16-62.

(10)   John B. Romeyn, Sermon delivered in the Presbyterian Church of Albany, N. Y., Sept. 8, 1808.

prosperity. "Many are the prophetic signs," said Lyman Beecher, in 1813,

which declare the rapid approach of that day. . . . . The false prophet is hastening to perdition. That wicked one hath appeared, whom the Lord will destroy with the breath of His coming. The day of His vengeance is wasting the earth. . . . . The angel having the everlasting gospel to preach to men, has begun his flight and, with trumpet sounding long and waxing loud, is calling on the nations to look unto Jesus and be saved. (11)

To a committee of the American Board of Commissioners for Foreign Missions appointed to draw up an address to the Christian public in 1811, the period was one of vengeance and of promise—vengeance to the foes of the elect, and promise to the redeemed. "Prophecy, history, and the present state of the world," they said,

seem to unite in declaring that the great pillars of the Papal and Mahometan impostures are now tottering to their fall. . . . . Now is the time for the followers of Christ to come forward boldly, and to engage earnestly in the great work of enlightening and reforming mankind. (12)

An old prophecy made by John Eliot, the apostle to the Indians in the seventeenth century, was believed to have found fulfillment in the European Wars. Eliot had said, "God will bring many nations into distress and perplexity, so that they may be forced unto the Scriptures; all governments will be shaken, that men may be forced at last to pitch upon that firm foundation, the Word of God." (13) What period seemed better to accord with such an apocalyptic utterance than that of the two decades following the outbreak of the French Revolution?

(11)   Lyman Beecher, Sermon delivered at New Haven, Oct. 27, 1813.
(12)   *Panoplist,* November, 1811. The committee comprised Jedidiah Morse, Samuel Worcester, and Jeremiah Evarts.
(13)   *The Adviser* or *Vermont Evangelical Magazine,* August, 1809.

Probably the most indefatigable defender of orthodoxy in New England was Jedidiah Morse, pastor of the Congregational Church at Charlestown, Mass. In 1810 Morse preached the annual sermon before the Society for Propagating the Gospel among the Indians and Others in North America. Taking for his text Daniel 12:4-10, he assured his audience that the Eastern and Western Antichrists—to be understood as the Turkish Empire and the Papacy—had both arisen in 606 and would therefore both disappear in 1866. Then the Jews would return to Palestine, the Gentiles would be converted, and the millenium would follow. The Napoleonic wars were preparing the way for the end. Recent maritime discoveries and explorations were a sure indication that the end of the age was at hand, because in Daniel it was said, with reference to the approach of the millenium, "Many shall run to and fro and knowledge shall be increased." The foundation of the Asiatic Society in 1784, to promote the study of Oriental antiquities was a clear fulfillment of prophecy. The rise of Bible societies and other agencies for diffusing Christian knowledge was ample evidence that the end of the age was drawing near. In view of the grandeur of the design and its relation to Bible prophecy the missionary enterprise deserved the zealous promotion of all Christians. The time was short. Much remained to be done within the fifty years that were left. (14)

The same confidence in the approaching end of the age was shared by Edward D. Griffin, pastor of the Park Street Church of Boston, in a sermon preached in Sandwich in 1813. The end of the papal regime might be expected not later than 1866. Quite possible was it that it would come in 1847 or 1848 if the twelve hundred and sixty prophetic years were reduced to Chaldean or solar years. If there remained any doubts concerning the accuracy of this construction of Biblical mathematics the revolutions

(14)   Jedidiah Morse, Discourse delivered before the Society for Propagating the Gospel among the Indians and Others in North America, November 1, 1810.

and wars taking place all over the earth ought to convince serious people that the end of the age was near. "So exactly do the events of the present day accord with the predictions, both in kind and in order, that we are enabled with some degree of certainty, to determine how far we are advanced under the seven vials." (15)

What have the prophecies to say about missions? Here Griffin was more explicit than most of his contemporaries.

> The most distinguished writers on the prophecies, though differing in other respects, have been constrained to agree . . . that in 1792, a new era opened to the world. . . . . That very year introduced the grand era of missions. The first missionary society of modern origin was formed in England in 1792. Since that time the whole concourse of missionary and Bible Societies . . . . have come into existence. . . . . Precisely at the commencement of this interesting era began . . . . those heavenly showers of grace [the American revivals] . . . . May we not then yield ourselves to the confidence that Zion has seen her darkest hour, and that her light will henceforth continue to shine with increasing brightness to the perfect day? (16)

The religious journals of the period, most of which were missionary magazines, joined in the all but universal chorus to the effect that a new era was about to begin. Infidelity would be dealt its death blow through the coming conversion and restoration of the Jews in fulfillment of prophecy. (17)   That Paul had the Age of Reason in mind in II Timothy 3-1-9 was evident from the close correspondence between his descriptions of society in the last days and the prevalence of infidelity and licentiousness in America. (18)   On the other hand, that efforts

(15)   Edward D. Griffin, Sermon preached in Sandwich, Mass., Oct. 20, 1813.
(16)   *Ibid.*
(17)   *Theological Magazine*, vol. iii, p. 123.
(18)   *Connecticut Evangelical Magazine*, Feb., 1801.

should be made during those fateful years, on a scale hitherto unimagined, for the purpose of evangelizing the heathen seemed all the more certainly to betoken the divine character of the missionary enterprise. (19) The revivals which characterized the age were alone sufficient to lead good men to tremble at the signs of the times. (20) It was no wonder that the hope was being indulged that the grand jubilee was at hand. (21)

Numerous were the passages in the Bible which were cited as proof that the Jews would accept the Christian religion and return to their old home in Palestine where the kingdom of David and Solomon would be revived. (22) That Israelites had been predestined to wander over the earth without a national home for a long period of time had been clear to Moses, their great lawygiver, and by other inspired writers of the Old Testament. Just as certainly had their conversion and restoration been foreseen by prophets of their own race, including the great apostle to the Gentiles, Paul of Tarsus. The conversion of the Jews would constitute a very important part of the approaching prosperity of the Church. It would, without doubt, be a prelude to the general acceptance of Christianity by the heathen peoples of the earth. The conversion of aborigines and pioneers through the efforts of the numerous missionary societies in the United States, during the early years of the nineteenth century, was signal proof that a new era was beginning. It was to be hoped that Jews in America might more readily accept the Messiah

(19) *New York Missionary Magazine,* 1802. Report of the Trustees of the Connecticut Missionary Society for June, 1802.

(20) *Connecticut Evangelical Magazine,* August, 1803. Analysis of the Book of Daniel.

(21) See Appendix.

(22) One such list was given in *The Connecticut Evangelical Magazine* for October, 1800. The most important passages according to the writer were: Gen. 17:8; Jer. 31:31, 34; Ezek. 34:11-14, 28, 29; Ezek. 37; Ezek. 39:28; Amos 9:14, 15; Hosea 3:14, 15; Zech. 12:10; 14:9-11; Luke 21:24; and Romans 11:1-26. John H. Livingston in a sermon preached before the New York Missionary Society, April 23, 1799, included several passages not in this list, notably Deut. 28:49-68, and 30:3-5.

than their brethren in Europe, because of the better treatment accorded the race in the New World. (23)

Missionary sermons during the early years of the nineteenth century reflected a widespread feeling of confidence in the imminent conversion of the Jews to Christianity. Samuel Spring of Newburyport in a missionary address in 1802 understood from his study of prophecy that the divine plan for reclaiming the world involved the restoration of the Jews as a consequence of the conversion of the Gentiles. (24) The exertion of Christians for the salvation of the Gentiles was therefore a necessary part in the fulfillment of prophecy concerning the Jews. Efforts should not be spared to reach both Jews and Gentiles in view of the intimate relation existing between them in Biblical prophecy. (25) Likewise, Nehemiah Prudden of Enfield, in a sermon before the Connecticut Missionary Society in 1805, was moved to ask:

> Is it not true that the heathen now testify that they are given the Son for his inheritance, and the uttermost parts of the earth for his possession? Is it not evident . . . . that the Euphrates is drying up, and the way preparing for the kings of the East to come in? That the time is approaching when the Jews shall have a hearing ear given them, and an understanding heart, and shall be

(23)   *Conn. Evan. Mag.,* Sept. and Nov., 1800; Joseph Eckley, Sermon before the Society for Propagating the Gospel among the Indians and Others in North America, Nov. 7, 1805.

(24)   Timothy Dwight likewise believed the conversion and restoration of the Jews would follow, not precede, the world wide dissemination of the gospel. "The Jews, provoked to jealousy, and roused from the torpor of eighteen centuries, shall behold a standard lifted up among the nations, and an ensign among the people, summoning them again to the land of their fathers, and to the Kingdom of God." (*Panoplist,* March, 1809. Sermon by Timothy Dwight at the opening of Andover Theological Seminary, Sept. 28, 1808).
On the other hand, John H. Livingston believed that the fulness of the Gentiles would come after the conversion and restoration of the Jews in accordance with his understanding of Roman 11:15. (J. H. Livingston's sermon before the N. Y. Miss. Soc., Apr. 3, 1804).

(25)   Samuel Spring, A sermon delivered before the Massachusetts Missionary Society at their annual meeting May 25, 1802.

gathered in with the fulness of the Gentiles, and the appearance of the world, in moral things, shall be like a new creation of God? (26)

The expectations of clergymen and missionary promoters that something unusual was about to occur, which would eventuate in the fulfillment of prophecy concerning the Jews, were considerably heightened by information from England telling of the organization in 1809 of the London Society for the Promotion of Christianity among the Jews, and the remarkable success attending the work of its founder, S. C. F. Frey, a converted German Jew. Frey's mission to the London Jews was given wide publicity through the American missionary journals, particularly *The Panoplist* and *The Connecticut Evangelical Magazine.* In 1815 a number of women in Boston and vicinity, who had become interested in Jewish missions through reading the story of Frey's career, associated and contributed fifty dollars to the London Jewish Society. The following year the Boston women organized "The Female Society of Boston and vicinity, for promoting Christianity among the Jews." (27) A similar organization was started in New York in 1816. The hopes of the Boston Society were expressed in their third annual report to the effect that the period was drawing near when the Jews, in accordance with prophecy, would accept the Messiah. All signs seemed to indicate beyond a doubt that the day was at hand. Means, however, had to be used, as God had nowhere promised to perform a miracle. Therefore, everyone interested was urged to help fulfill prophecy by supporting the Jewish mission. All money raised was being sent to London to be used for the evangelization of Jews there. (28)

Buchanan's sermon "The Star in the East" was published in an American edition at Cambridge, Mass., by the Society of Inquiry at Andover. (29) It was epoch making in its effects be-

(26) Sermon by Nehemiah Prudden of Enfield, Conn., before the Miss. Soc. of Conn., at Hartford, May 9, 1805. *Conn. Evan. Mag.,* July, 1805.
(27) *American Baptist Magazine,* Jan., 1817.
(28) *Panoplist,* Oct., 1816 and July, 1819.
(29) *Memoir of American Missionaries.*

cause it stirred up the missionary zeal of many young men in the denominational colleges and at Andover. The author, an Anglican chaplain, had traveled extensively in Asia. He sought to bring to the attention of Christendom the stir that was being made in the Asiatic world, largely as a consequence of the Napoleonic wars. The Jews, he believed, were about to accept Christianity. Scattered over the earth, in accordance with Scripture prophecy, they were at last giving attention to those passages in holy writ, particularly the oracles of Isaiah, which dealt with their future as a nation. Other Oriental peoples were being aroused to study the prophecies, so that ere long, he felt, every nation would understand the divine decrees concerning itself. In Europe, France which had first seduced the Catholic countries by her infidelity had at last become the instrument of their punishment. After the seat of the inquisition had been sufficiently purged with blood to satisfy the demands of divine justice, great changes for the better might be expected. If anyone desired evidence for this optimistic expectation it could be found in the new interest being shown in missions to the heathen. Other signs of the times were the fulfillment of Biblical prophecy in world events, particularly in the universal prevalence of war; the translation of the Scriptures into the languages of the East Indians; and the efforts of infidelity to check the spread of the gospel. All of these signs, taken together, warranted the belief that the millenium was at hand. (30)

Joseph Harvey, the Congregational minister of Goshen, Conn., preached the annual sermon before the Foreign Mission Society of Litchfield County in 1815. He believed that the time of the end was clearly drawing near. He assured his audience that they were living in the "last days." "Most writers on the prophecies," he said, "have fixed the commencement of the millenium somewhere near the seventh thousand year of the world, or the year two thousand of the Christian era. No calculations,

---

(30)   *Evangelical Intelligencer,* July and Aug., 1809. Quotations from Buchanan's *Star in the East.*

I believe, have carried the millenium beyond this point, though some have come short of it." The Church of Rome, he understood, was scheduled to flourish from 606 to 1866. In the latter year it would fall, along with the Turkish Empire, and the Jews would be restored to Palestine. "Within about fifty years hence, then, we may expect the fall of mystical Babylon, the drying-up of the river Euphrates, or the extinction of Mohammedanism, and the restoration of the ancient people of God." At the same time Harvey believed the secular enemies of the church would meet their doom and the battle of Armageddon would be fought. Great and continuous revivals such as had not been experienced by the church since its earliest days, together with a missionary spirit hitherto undreamed of, betokened the nearness of the "day of glory." "In the present calamities of the world," he concluded, "we see nothing but what had been fully predicted." It was the urgent duty of all Christians to "consider the nearness of the latter day glory, and the shortness of the time in which the great work is to be done." (31)

The Concert of Prayer was a very prominent aspect of the missionary movement on both sides of the Atlantic. It was also utilized by missionaries in Asia, Africa, and the South Seas. (32) Its origin is obscure, but it was in use in the West of Scotland as early as 1744. As practiced there by some clergymen a portion of Saturday evening and Sunday morning was set apart each week, and also the first Tuesday of February, May, August, and November, as special periods appointed for private or public prayer for the progress of the Kingdom of God. Five hundred copies of a memorial published in 1746, explaining the idea, found their way to New England. The following year Jonathan Edwards first published an account of the Concert entitled, "An humble attempt to promote explicit agreement and visible union of God's people in

(31)   Joseph Harvey, Sermon preached at Litchfield, pp. 6-27.

(32)   Extracts from the Minutes of the General Assembly of the Presbyterian Church in the United States of America, 1815; H. L. Osgood, *The American Colonies in the Eighteenth Century,* vol. iii, pp. 437, 438.

extraordinary prayer for the Revival of Religion, and the advancement of Christ's Kingdom on earth, pursuant to Scripture promises and prophecies concerning the last time." (33)

No direct result followed the publication of Edwards's book, but an English edition of it appeared in 1789 and served to influence the Particular Baptist ministers of the Northampton and Leicestershire associations, who had adopted a plan for a concert of prayer, five years before, and who because of the interest in world evangelization engendered by the concert and by Edwards's book were led to organize, in 1792, the Particular Baptist Society for the Propagation of the Gospel among the Heathen. The English plan for a concert provided that the first Monday of each month be set apart as a special day to pray for the universal spread of the gospel. (34)

In 1794 the first successful effort to put into practice a concert plan in America was made as a result of a meeting of clergymen at Lebanon, Conn., who sent out invitations to ministers and congregations throughout the country to join in concerted prayer on the first Tuesday of every quarter of the year, beginning in January, 1795, at two o'clock in the afternoon. (35) During the next few years concerts were begun in various parts of the land, although no agreement was reached among the various missionary societies which would make for uniformity of method or of specified times for concerted prayer. By 1816 the first Monday of every month was the appointed time most generally observed. (36)

The fulfillment of prophecy through the conversion of Jews and heathen and the hastening of the millenium was the burden

(33)   John Campbell, *Maritime Discovery and Christian Missions*, pp. 159, 160.

(34)   *Second Annual Report of the Baptist Board of Foreign Missions*, p. 81.

(35)   Wm. Linn, *Discourses on the Signs of the Times*, pp. 174, 175.

(36)   *Conn. Evan. Mag.*, Feb., 1801. Letter from Rev. Ammi R. Robbins of Norfolk, Conn.; *New York Miss. Mag.*, 1800, pp. 50, 51; 89-94; *Ibid.*, 1801, pp. 452, 453; Extracts from the Minutes of the Gen. Assembly of the Presby. Ch., 1816; *Second Annual Rep. of the Bap. Bd. F. M.*, p. 81.

of the petitions offered on these occasions of special prayer. (37)
It was even felt that the concert itself was a fulfillment of prophecy. (38) In view of the manifest fulfillment in contemporary
world events of a part of Daniel 12:4 which reads: "Many shall
run to and fro, and knowledge shall be increased," it seemed
eminently fitting and proper that people should pray that the
Kingdom of God might come speedily. (39) Joseph Badger, a
missionary to the Wyandot Indians, in a letter written to Jedidiah
Morse in 1809, voiced the current feeling about the close relation
between prophecy and prayer for the heathen when he said: "The
salvation of the heathen is so fully brought into view in Scripture
prophecy, that it is ardently requested of the friends of Zion to
pray for the accomplishment of such a glorious event." (40)
Praying societies everywhere were praising the great head of the
Church for sending the gospel to pagan idolaters and for shower-
ing the country with blessings in the form of most unusual
revivals of religion. It was but natural that they should continue

(37) *Panoplist*, Jan., 1809.
(38) *Conn. Evan. Mag.*, Aug., 1803.
(39) *Piscataqua Evangelical Magazine*, July, August, Sept., and Octo-
      ber, 1805. Article, "The Progress of the Gospel."
(40) *Panoplist*, Feb., 1809. Report of Joseph Badger to Jedidiah
      Morse on his work among the Wyandot Indians.
          A resolution adopted at the time of the formation of the Evan-
      gelical Society of Pennsylvania, a Presbyterian missionary and tract
      society, in 1808, recommended that the hour next succeeding the
      rising of the sun each Sunday morning be given by all members
      as a period of concerted prayer for the progress of Christianity
      and the prevalence of good-will on earth. It read: "Resolved un-
      animously to recommend . . . . that the hour, or part of the
      hour, next succeeding to the rising of the sun on every Sabbath
      morning, be occupied by individual members in praise to the Great
      Head of the church, for His goodness in sending the Gospel to
      many of the human family wholly devoted to idolatry; for so
      much unanimity among His people in the efforts which have been
      directed to this object; for reviving His cause in several parts of
      this continent; and also in importunate prayer to Almighty God,
      beseeching a continuance of His blessing; that He would send
      forth more laborers into His vineyard with increasing success; that
      the various commotions in the world may be overruled for the
      advantage of the Redeemer's Kingdom, the increase of knowledge,
      true catholicism, Christian charity, and liberty of conscience."
      (*Panoplist*, Jan., 1809).

to besiege the divine throne in the earnest hope that Jews and Gentiles would accept Christianity and that the great day of millenial bliss would soon dawn.

Missionary propaganda became increasingly effective during the early years of the nineteenth century as a means of turning the defensive attitude of Christians toward infidel philosophy into a crusade against the enemies of the gospel. Through the interpretation of the sure word of prophecy by countless students of the Scriptures it was made abundantly clear that many hitherto obscure passages in the Bible were about to be unveiled. Infidelity would be silenced, the Jews convinced of the truth of the Christian religion, and Gentiles saved. Through the organization of praying societies the millenium was being substantially hastened. It became the welcome task of the zealous advocates of missions to meet all conceivable objections which might be raised against the evangelization of the Jews and the heathen and to make understandable to all who could be reached that missions ought to be supported by prayer and money. Sermons, tracts, and missionary magazines were the mediums of this propaganda. The popularization of the world wide missionary enterprise was the outstanding achievement of its advocates.

The spirit of Old Calvinism which lingered on for some time after Edwards and Whitefield had delivered it a death wound was antagonistic to missionary propaganda. The suggestion of the use of human agencies for the advancement of Christianity seemed presumption. God would convert the pagan world and the Jews when and in what manner he pleased. This had been Calvin's attitude, and it remained, with some notable exceptions, the attitude of his followers, down to the time of the Great Awakening. The refutation of this Old Calvinism was a task which the new generation of leaders, trained in the theology of Edwards, Hopkins, Witherspoon, and Tennent, eagerly sought.

In the same year that William Carey published his *Enquiry into the obligations of Christians to use means for the conversion of the heathens,* Shippie Townsend preached a sermon in Boston in which he essayed to prove to the Old Calvinists that the doctrine of election did not militate against the use of means for the salvation of souls. The elect were under obligations to the unsaved, and it behooved them to preach the gospel and leave the matter of their ultimate salvation to God. Among those to whom the elect were especially obligated were the Jews. Pure gratitude to God because of one's election ought to suffice as an incentive to propagate the gospel among sinners everywhere. (41) The rapid spread of Hopkinsianism served as a most potent leaven to transform the attitude of Calvinists generally from one of indifference or unconcern into a burning zeal for the conversion of the unsaved in all parts of the world. The most formidable obstacle to the missionary propagandist was the lethargy of Christians who had no theoretical objection whatever to the enterprise, but who could with great difficulty be persuaded to contribute to the cause. It was the task of arousing this great body of indifferent church members to a sense of responsibility for the heathen that required the expenditure of a great amount of energy on the part of the missionary enthusiasts. Various were the appeals made from the pulpit and through tracts and missionary journals in the new crusade to advance the frontiers of the Kingdom of God.

That the heathen were doomed to everlasting torture in hell unless reached by Christian missionaries was considered a theological axiom. Should God in some mysterious way and for some unknown purpose elect to save some of them, there was, nevertheless, every reason to believe that the great majority of them would be lost. Christians might well beware then lest they too perish through inactivity and indifference.

Suppose in that dreadful day some miserable condemned pagan just ready to sink into the eternal flames should turn his despairing eyes upon you and exclaim in a voice that shall rend your heart; 'Why, why did you not warn me of this day? Why did you not exhort me to flee from this vengeance.' (42)

(41)   Shippie Townsend, The Gospel considered; and the manner in which it should be preached.
(42)   Henry Kolloch, Sermon before the General Assembly of the Presbyterian Church in the U. S. A., May 23, 1803.

Warnings of this sort served to arouse the indifferent Christian through an appeal to his fear of the judgment.

The exertions being made by the British missionary societies during the darkest hours of their nation's struggle with Napoleon seemed to missionary zealots to be nothing less than a rebuke to the citizens of a nation which could boast of the services of Eliot, Brainerd, Edwards, and the Mayhews. Even though Britain might be atoning for her former sins she seemed now to be revealing her true character as a genuine Christian nation in seeking to extend the Redeemer's kingdom, so that offers of pardon were being made "to the stupid Hottentot, the credulous Hindu, and the wandering Tartar." Prayers for England's protection were ascending "from the Cape of Good Hope to where the Ganges rolls its waves." Americans would do well to emulate their British brethren in this worthy enterprise. (43) The appeal to the pride of Americans in view of their increasing consciousness of nationality constituted an important factor in developing missionary enthusiasm.

In the light of the widespread feeling that the time had arrived when obscure Scripture prophecies concerning the last days were beginning to find their fulfillment in current events, the Great Commission of Christ, as stated in Matt. 28:19 and Mark 16:15 took on a new meaning. It was quite generally conceded that the Protestant churches had been remiss in that they had, for the most part, neglected a specific command. An ardent desire to atone for the indifference of past generations of Christians seized possession of whole groups of young men in some of the newly established colleges, particularly in Williams, Middlebury and Union. Adoniram Judson, while a student at Andover Theological Seminary felt the force of the divine command and enlisted as one of America's first foreign missionaries. The field was far distant, and the climate was unhealthy. He was almost

(43)   *Panoplist*, May, 1809, p. 553.

disheartened as he thought of the prospect. But the last great command of Christ determined him to obey "at all hazards for the sake of pleasing the Lord Jesus Christ." (44)

Samuel Nott, another of the young men first sent out by the American Board testified to the impelling power of the sense of duty experienced by these early missionaries. There was nothing involved which could be termed a spirit of romance or adventure. It was rather piety taking the direction of missions. (45)   The conviction that Christians owed their Master a duty, primarily the duty of implicit obedience, was strongly felt not only by those who carried the gospel to foreign lands, but also by those who were called upon to finance the enterprise from the home base, and who were expected to pray for its success. Missionary propaganda stressed the idea of duty, the duty of a soldier to take his marching orders without question.

The Hopkinsian idea of disinterested benevolence, the doctrine that for the greater glory of God the elect should joyfully engage in any service, however otherwise distasteful, that would add to the sum total of happiness of "being in general," was rapidly supplanting the Old Calvinist attitude of unconcern for human misery and wretchedness. Joseph Eckley in a sermon before the Boston S. P. G. in 1805 developed the well known Hopkinsian tenets that man's redemption was transcendently glorious among the works of God, that the good resulting from Christ's atoning death was so great as to completely absorb the idea of evil and to afford to God Himself the perfect enjoyment of infinite felicity, and that not a single event, at any time, among any beings, or in any world, was incapable of being subjected to the designs of infinite benevolence. (46)   Such a philosophy of life, slowly permeating as it did, the theological thought of New Eng-

(44)   Edward Judson, *Life of Adoniram Judson*, p. 474.
(45)   *Memorial volume of the first fifty years of the American Board of Commissioners for Foreign Missions*, p. 54.
(46)   *Panoplist*, Aug., 1806, Sermon by Joseph Eckley, Nov. 7, 1805, before the Society for Propagating the Gospel among the Indians and Others in North America.

land, might well be expected to produce a new generation of Christian martyrs. Altruism, that is, benevolence which expects no recompense, came into the foreground of all the appeals which missionary propagandists were making for the support of the project of world evangelization.

The missionary cause according to Leonard Woods of Andover Theological Seminary was the cause of Christ in relation to the whole unevangelized world. Though the particular appeal below cited was voiced a decade after the organization of the American Board, its sentiments are not inappropriately applied to the earlier situation. "It seems impossible," said Woods, that any man who considers the Christian religion a blessing should not desire its universal diffusion. Objections against the missionary cause are consistent enough from the mouths of deists and atheists; but for Christians to make them is a shocking absurdity. . . . . Think of the difference between the inhabitants of New England, and the people in those countries where pagan influence prevails. To what is all the difference owing, but to the Christian religion?

What a glorious scene would be witnessed at some future date with all these pagan idolaters converted and their children listening with weeping tenderness to the voice of Christian instruction. (47) Here was propaganda appealing to the imagination. The whole world was to become an enlarged Puritan New England!

To save countless millions of heathen from everlasting punishment, to emulate their British brethren in their heroic efforts to evangelize the world, to obey the Great Commission which had enjoined missions on a universal scale, and to put into practice the principle of disinterested benevolence out of pure love to God and to all "beings capable of good," were the most conspicuously stressed motives for Christians to engage in Foreign Missions. But acting as a dynamic back of these motives was

(47)   Leonard Woods, Sermon delivered July 12, 1821, in the Tabernacle Church of Salem on the occasion of the death of Rev. Samuel Worcester.

the all but universal conviction that Bible prophecies clearly referred to events which were transpiring. The early years of the nineteenth century seemed to Bible students to have been foreshadowed as the day of the gospel. Missionary propagandists did not neglect their duty in this regard. Slumbering saints could be aroused to action, in many instances, by nothing less than the reiteration of the current belief that the millenium was near. *The Piscataqua Evangelical Magazine* was moved in 1805 to make an appeal to Christians of every denomination in an effort to bring them to realize that the gospel had not yet been spread to the extent that prophecy indicated would be true shortly before the millenium. Only a small portion of the earth, by comparison, had acknowledged the Christian religion in any form whatever. Both in Europe and America, however, extraordinary exertions were being made to remedy this sad condition, and it was hoped that the time to favor Zion had at last come. (48)

Of 800,000,000 human beings on earth, said *The Massachusetts Missionary Magazine* in 1803, only about 50,000,000 were Protestant Christians. 500,000,000 were pagans and 250,000,000 were Mohammedans, Jews, and Papists. But Christians during the decade past had been roused from their slumbers and were now to be found laboring to save the heathen in India, Africa, and the South Seas. (49) *The Panoplist* in 1806 printed a letter from William Carey to a friend in Edinburgh in which he stated that three-quarters of the wealth which God had committed to His Church was being withheld for all sorts of trivial reasons. Few people realized, said Carey, the awful sin of not devoting all their talents, influence, and substance to the Lord. £250,000 would be needed to furnish every twelfth person in Bengal with a New Testament. (50) Still, despite all the handicaps involved through the timidity of Christians in their philanthropy, it was rapidly becoming evident that progress was being made.

(48) *Piscataqua Evangelical Magazine,* Jan. and Feb., 1805
(49) *Mass. Miss. Mag.,* June, 1803, p. 65.
(50) *Panoplist,* Aug., 1806. Letter of William Carey to a friend in Edinburgh, Sept. 27, 1804.

The revolutions among the nations and the judgments of God upon wicked governments seemed to the General Association of ministers of New Hampshire at their annual meeting in 1809 to betoken the universal spread of the gospel. Speaking of missionary exertions their report urged that no one plead the want of talents or opportunity to promote the cause. Everyone could do something. "There is none who cannot cast in his mite." (51) With good reason could *The Panoplist*, that ardent defender of religion, pure and undefiled, rejoice:

This is the day of great events, both in the civil and religious world. The King of Kings is fast preparing the way for the final consummation. The scene is coming to a close. From the prophecies of Scripture and the motions of divine providence, we are led to expect that the day of Zion's enlargement, beauty, and joy draws near. Let us be resolute, active, and constant in advancing the kingdom of grace; and lift up our heads with rejoicing in prospect of the kingdom of glory. (52)

Appeals of this sort were designed to arouse people who needed to be assured that the cause was headed straight for victory. Nothing succeeds like success.

On February 6, 1812 the first American missionaries to a foreign land were ordained in Salem. Leonard Woods of Andover Theological Seminary preached the sermon on that occasion. Six outstanding motives for the propagation of Christianity among the heathen were discussed. They were: the worth of souls; the plenteous provision made for human redemption through the death of Christ; the command to spread the gospel; the example of the apostles; the universal applicability of the gospel; and Scripture prophecy. In reference to the last item Woods felt that there was every reason to be optimistic. Better

(51)   *Panoplist*, Dec., 1809, pp. 329, 330.
(52)   *Panoplist*, August, 1809.

things were just ahead. The millenial glory of the church was about to be ushered in. The realization of victory, he believed would act as an incentive to greater activity on the part of American Christians. (53)

(53) Sermon by Leonard Woods delivered in Salem, Feb. 6, 1812, at the ordination of Newell, Judson, Nott, Hall, and Rice.

CHAPTER VII

DISINTERESTED BENEVOLENCE

The missionary spirit in its onward rush was not restricted to a single channel. Evangelical missions to pioneers, Indians, and pagan peoples overseas constituted but one phase of a movement which was missionary in a larger sense. The rise of tract (1) and Bible societies, (2) Sunday Schools, (3) and orphanages, (4) followed by the organization of asylums for deaf mutes, (5) the American Colonization Society for Free Negroes, (6) soci-

---

(1) For an account of the work of the Religious Tract Society of Great Britain see *Mass. Miss. Mag.*, Jan., 1807, and *Pan.*, Dec., 1805. For an account of the formation of the Massachusetts Society for Promoting Christian Knowledge see *Pan.*, July, 1807, and *Mass. Miss. Mag.*, Mch., 1808. For the Connecticut Religious Tract Society see *Pan.*, Sept., 1807. For the history of tract societies in America see Fifth Annual Report of the New England Tract Society, in *Religious Intelligencer* Oct. 16, 1819.

(2) For periodical accounts of the work of British and American Bible Societies see especially *Pan.*, Aug., 1805; Oct., 1807; *Evan. Intell.*, Jan., 1809; May, 1809; *Vt. Evan. Mag.*, Feb., 1809; *Boston Recorder*, Feb. 14, 1816; *Am. Bap. Mag.*, Jan., 1817.

(3) Extracts from the Minutes of the Gen. Assembly Presby. Ch., 1816.

(4) For Boston Female Asylum see *N. Y. Miss. Mag.*, 1801, pp. 381-385; for Female Charitable Society of Salem, see sermon by Moses Stuart before the Society, 1815; for Ladies Society in New York for relief of poor widows with children, see *N. Y. Miss. Mag.*, Jan., 1803; for account of Savannah Female Asylum see *Georgia Analytical Repository*, vol. i, pp. 68-74.

(5) Emerson Davis, The Half Century.

(6) For Formation of the African Institution of London see *Pan.*, Nov., 1807. For Hopkins and the Colonization movement see Hopkins, *Works*, vol. ii, pp. 610-612. For Colonization Society see A. Alexander, *History of Colonization;* Extracts from Minutes of Presby. Ch., 1819; I. V. Brown, *Memoir of Robert Finley, passim.*

eties for the suppression of vice and intemperance, (7) and other similar societies designed to improve the celestial and terrestrial welfare of unfortunate human beings, testified to the awakening of the benevolent and humanitarian spirit. In America, at the outset, the movement was, for the most part, religious in character, although there was not wanting a non-religious humanitarianism inspired by men of the type of Jefferson and Thomas Paine. Democratic individualism as preached by Jefferson reinforced the religious movement in that it heightened the value of the common man. Wesleyan Methodism made a more significant contribution through its emphasis on the infinite love and pity of God and the incalculable worth of immortal souls. It was Hopkinsian Calvinism, however, that made the most effective contributions to the cause of disinterested benevolence in that it furnished men and missionary machinery for carrying the gospel to the Far East, to Africa and to the South Seas.

The theological jargon of Samuel Hopkins is almost a foreign language to a twentieth century reader. Yet the humanitarian gospel of Puritanism as it was received and preached by the early missionaries was a by-product of some of Hopkins's peculiar theological tenets, and one must needs understand something of that theology in order properly to evaluate the services of an Adoniram Judson or a Samuel J. Mills. Hopkinsianism, among other things, included some peculiar ideas about man's relation to his future destiny. According to Hopkins there were plenty of Old Calvinists who could anticipate the damnation of their non-elect neighbors with considerable satisfaction, because the sovereignity of God would in such cases be demonstrated. Those same worthy men, however, were quite naturally not enthusiastic in contemplating the possibility of their own eternal torment as a factor in strengthening the divine government. Hopkins, on the other hand, maintained that one must be willing,

---

(7) For English Society for the Suppression of Vice, see *Pan.*, July, 1808. For Massachusetts Society, see sermon by Lyman Beecher, Oct. 12, 1812, New Haven; see also J. A. Krout, *Origins of Prohibition*, chap. 5.

nay even anxious to spend his eternity in hell if it should chance
to please God to send him there. (8) He and his followers were
styled Consistent Calvinists in that they carried the idea of sub-
mission to the sovereign will of God to an extent that could be
matched only in some of the most extreme of the medieval mys-
tics. Truly it required heroism to be a Consistent Calvinist.

In willingness to endure hardship as soldiers of the cross,
Hopkinsians were in no respect inferior to the Wesleyan Methodists. Both resembled the earlier Jesuit missionaries. But the
followers of Hopkins had as an avowed motive for their activity
a totally different theological concept from that of the Methodists. The idea that the love of the redeemed sinner for God
originated in the realization that God first loved mankind and was
seeking to save all sinners — an idea popularized by Wesley
and his followers — Hopkins denounced as false, in that it
excluded "benevolent affection" for God regardless of His plans
for mankind. Said Hopkins on this point: "He who has a new
heart, and universal disinterested benevolence will be a friend
to God . . . . though he see not the least evidence . . . . that
God loves him and designs to save him. . . . . The benevolent
Christian rejoices independent of his own interest, in the hope
and assurance of the glory of God." (9)   Before a person can
have any assurance that he is saved he must first have what Hopkins so frequently styles "disinterested benevolence." (10)

The objects upon which the Christian should practice the
principle of disinterested benevolence included "all beings which
exist, capable of good, or that can be in any sense or degree,
objects of good-will." Since the highest good of the whole was
the design of God in creating the world, the highest degree of
happiness to the greatest possible number of creatures ought to
be the chief concern of the Christian. (11)   The earthly goal
of such efforts as Consistent Calvinists might properly seek to

(8)   Hopkins *Works,* vol. i, p. 211.
(9)   *Ibid.,* vol. i, pp. 386-399.
(10)   *Ibid.,* vol. iii, p. 62.
(11)   *Ibid.,* vol. iii, p. 16.

achieve was described by Hopkins and may be regarded as the Hopkinsian Utopia. For Hopkinsians were not altogether other-worldly in their philosophy. "Whenever Christianity shall have spread over the whole world," said Hopkins,

and the distinguishing spirit and power of it take place universally, forming to a high degree of universal benevolence and disinterested affection, it will unite mankind into one happy society, teaching them to love one another as brethren, each one seeking and rejoicing in the public good and in the happiness of individuals: this will form the most happy state of public society that can be enjoyed on earth. . . . . And they will hereby be made meet for the eternal inheritance of the saints in light. (12)

A letter from Hopkins to Andrew Fuller, the Secretary of the English Baptist Missionary Society, written in 1796 told of the growth of the Hopkinsian movement and indicated something of the importance it was coming to have in American theological circles. Hopkins said:

About forty years ago there were but few, perhaps not more than four or five, who espoused the sentiments which since have been called Edwardean, and New Divinity; and since, after some improvement was made upon them, Hopkintonian, or Hopkinsian sentiments. But these sentiments have so spread since that time among ministers . . . . that there are now more than one hundred who espouse the same sentiments, in the United States of America.

The number of Hopkinsians, according to the letter, was still rapidly increasing. (13)

Among the Hopkinsian ministers there was Daniel Hopkins, a brother of Samuel, who was pastor of the Third Congregational Church of Salem, Mass., the church of which John Norris was

(12)   *Ibid.*, vol. i, p. 399.
(13)   *Ibid.*, vol. i, pp. 237-238.

a member. Through his pastor, Norris became acquainted with Samuel Hopkins and took great pleasure in the thought that Hopkinsianism would be taught at Andover, the seminary which he helped to endow. To Norris the missionary idea was practically synonymous with Hopkinsian disinterested benevolence. (14)

Of course not all Hopkinsians were as extreme as Hopkins, especially in some of his more peculiar tenets. That there was a general agreement, however, with his theory of disinterested benevolence was evident in the willingness of his disciples to sacrifice comfort, position, friends, country, even life itself, for the sake of the ideas in which they had been steeped from infancy. The stern sense of duty drove men to attempt the impossible. It was duty that Adoniram Judson stressed as the motive which impelled him to go to the East. (15)   Samuel J. Mills was likewise a consistent disciple of Hopkins. So close was the intimacy between the Mills family and the Newport pastor that a copy of Hopkins's colonization scheme was sent to Torringford when Samuel J. Mills, Jr. was a small boy. Mills died in 1818 while in the service of the African Colonization Society. The intensity of Mills's zeal for the conversion of sinners was an inner urge which never for a moment left him in doubt as to his duty. He felt that he could conceive of no course in life which would prove so soul-satisfying as to carry the gospel to the "poor heathen." (16)   The record Mills left of his work among the poor and neglected of New York, Philadelphia, and Washington reveals the psychology of the Hopkinsian. Suffering humanity was clearly a challenge to the disinterested benevolence of Christians. The wretchedness that young Mills saw, however, was poverty of soul. The people were destitute, but the saddest destitution was the lack of the word of life. Bibles and religious literature must therefore be rushed to the aid of these ignorant

(14)   *Ibid.,* vol. i, p. 56.
(15)   Edward Judson, *Life of Adoniram Judson,* p. 474.
(16)   Gardiner Spring, *Memoir of S. J. Mills,* pp. 10-13;
        Hopkins, *Works,* vol. i, p. 164.

sinners. Suffering of a bodily sort, Mills, like many another "social worker" of his day, saw but regarded as of secondary importance. (17)

In the early years of the nineteenth century "social service" was, for the most part, a by-product of Methodist and Calvinist theological systems. Among the followers of Wesley the dominant emotion was that of pity for the ruined condition of the major portion of the human race. The great need of mankind was conceived to be the acceptance by the sinner of the pardon so freely offered by a loving God. Calvinism, on the other hand, particularly as it was interpreted by Hopkins, stressed the idea of duty. Whether or not the preaching of the gospel and the offer of a helping hand to suffering humanity were likely to prove effective, it was nevertheless the duty of Christians to practice disinterested benevolence. Of course there can be no absolute separation of the Calvinist and Methodist attitudes toward mankind. The former were coming to regard the atonement as general rather than limited to the elect. The latter as a matter of course had a rigid sense of duty. The Methodist circuit rider who felt under moral obligations to obey the orders of his superior without murmur quite naturally thought of his task as one involving duties to God and man. Still there continued to exist between the two groups a theological and emotional gulf of sufficient breadth to justify our regarding them as decidedly different. Particularly is this true in regard to their contributions to the missionary cause and to the progress of the spirit of humanitarianism.

In was the Calvinist influence rather than that of Wesleyan Methodism which made possible the extension of American Christianity to lands across the seas. As the young enthusiastic disciples of Edwards and Hopkins went into the waste places and jungles of the world, they went determined to lift mankind to a higher and a better plane of living. Even though the vast majority of mankind, in the opinion of the missionaries, was

(17)   Spring, *Memoir of S. J. Mills,* pp. 89-108.

destined to spend an eternity of excruciating and indescribable torment for the greater glory of God, still disinterested benevolence might well be the outstanding characteristic of all who had reason to believe themselves numbered among the elect. Duty required that they labor in heroic and unselfish service for the terrestrial as well as the celestial welfare of all creatures "capable of good." It was not romance, nor was it primarily the spirit of adventure that impelled them to leave friends and kindred and go to inhospitable lands, there to suffer privation and perhaps martyrdom. Their ideal of duty was the real impelling force. They were under obligations to act, not in accordance with their own interests, but in harmony with the spirit of disinterested benevolence. Their tasks were embraced with a joyous abandon that would have done credit to a medieval saint or a Jesuit missionary. No mercenary spirit or feeling that either in this life nor in the life to come an appropriate reward would ultimately be theirs seems to have motivated them, although it would be difficult to imagine the young Hopkinsian succeeding altogether in his efforts to uproot and cast utterly aside the idea of a heavenly reward as in some sense a recompense for sufferings and trials undergone on earth. They sought to take the best America then had to offer to the heathen world. It is by the standard of their faithfulness to their ideal of disinterested benevolence that they must be judged by a generation that finds it impossible to accept their theology.

APPENDIX

NOTE 21, CHAPTER 6, PAGE 131

As illustrative of the feeling in missionary circles toward contemporary events in their relation to prophecy a few more citations are here given:

"We know that it is the will of God the gospel should be preached to every creature. . . . . Scripture promises are in themselves a sufficient foundation for faith and hope, and for the most vigorous exertion. But the providences of God, at present, in a particular manner, concur with these promises, and afford ground to hope that their accomplishment draws nigh. Amid the tumults and confusions of war, a missionary spirit has been poured out in the European world, especially in Great Britain." (John McKnight, Sermon before the N. Y. Miss. Soc., Apr. 24, 1799, p. 55).

"The most respectable interpreters of the prophetic Scriptures have generally agreed in assigning the present as a highly interesting and eventful period. Their remarkable coincidence of system, in viewing these perilous times as introductory to the latter day glory, should be treated with respect, even by the most incredulous. It is no small token for good, in this respect, that so many in the Christian world are so anxiously looking and so earnestly praying for that happy day." (*New York Missionary Magazine*, 1800, p. 3).

"A coalition has been recently formed amongst Christians of various denominations, both in Europe and America, to propagate the gospel to distant nations. Their pious zeal has stimulated them to uncommon exertion, and the spirit of their Master has inspired them with the noble purpose of forgetting their partial distinctions for a higher and far more important object. This extraordinary union, and its attendant circumstances, are a happy presage, that the time approaches when according to the predictions of ancient prophecy, 'The nations shall fear the Lord from the West, and his glory from the rising sun.' " (*New York Missionary Magazine*, 1800, p. 104, *et seq.*, Address of the Northern Missionary Society in the State of New York to the public).

"For some years previous to the establishment of the Missionary Society of London. [London Missionary Society established 1795], the attention of many serious clergymen and other pious people had been turned to the subject of diffusing the gospel among Heathen Nations. Several passages in the prophecies of the Holy Scripture, together with the singular revolutions which were taking place among Christian nations—revolutions in sentiment as well as manners and government, induced serious, reflecting people to believe that Divine Providence was about to introduce some great change in the religious state of the world; and particularly that the time was approaching when 'the fulness of the Gentiles was to be gathered in.' " (*Conn. Evan. Mag.*, July, 1800, p. 7).

"Shall we not discuss the signs of the times, and derive encouragement from the providence and promises of God? Has He not at this period, awakened, in many parts of Protestant Christendom, an uncommon attention to the state of the heathen, and to greater exertions for the propagation of the gospel, than hath ever before been, since the age of the apostles? Can it be imagined that He is doing this without some wise

153

and glorious end, which He is about to answer? Does it not carry an intimation, that the time is about to commence, in which He will give to His son, the Heathen for His inheritance and the uttermost parts of the earth for His possession?" (*Conn. Evan. Mag.*, Sept., 1800, p. 91).

"Never, perhaps, since the apostolic age, has there been among Christians so general a zeal, such spirited and general exertions to advance the Kingdom of Jesus, and to bring all nations to the acknowledgement of the truth as it is in Him. While we contemplate these great and pleasing events,—may we not conclude that He is about to do something important and signal for His Church? Will He not arise and have mercy upon Zion? Is not the time to favor her, yea, the set time come?" (*N. Y. Miss. Mag.*, 1802, Report of the Trustees of the Conn. Miss. Society, June, 1802).

"Scripture prophecy leads us to hope for greater and more frequent revivals of religion than have been usual in past ages." The favorable events which led the writer to believe that important prophecies were about to be fulfilled were the missionary spirit in Europe and America and the revival of experimental religion in Europe and America. He concludes: "Even so good men tremble at the signs of the times at present." (*Conn. Evan. Mag.*, Aug., 1803, Analysis of the Book of Daniel).

BIBLIOGRAPHY

PERIODICALS

The Adviser or Vermont Evangelical Magazine, 7 vols., Middlebury, Vt., 1809-1815.

The American Monthly Review, 1 vol., Philadelphia, Jan.-Dec., 1795.

The American Moral and Sentimental Magazine, 1 vol., New York, July 3, 1797-May 21, 1798.

The American Universal Magazine, 4 vols., Philadelphia, Jan. 2, 1797-March 7, 1798.

The Analytical Repository (Georgia), vol. i, Savannah, 1802.

The Boston Magazine, Old Series, 3 vols; new series, 1 vol., Boston, October 30, 1802-April 26, 1805.

The Boston Recorder, Old Series, 1 vol., Boston, Jan. 3-Dec. 24, 1816.

The Christian Disciple, Boston, 1813-1824.

Connecticut Evangelical Magazine, 15 vols., Hartford, 1800-1814.

The General Assembly's Missionary Magazine or Evangelical Intelligencer, Old Series, 2 vols., new series, 3 vols., Philadelphia, 1805-1809.

The General Repository, 2 vols., Boston, 1812-1813.

Massachusetts Baptist Missionary Magazine, Boston, Sept., 1803-Dec., 1816.

Massachusetts Missionary Magazine, Boston, 1803-1808. (United with *Panoplist* in 1808).

The Monthly Anthology, Boston, 1803-1811.

The New York Missionary Magazine, 4 vols., New York, 1800-1803.

The Panoplist or The Christian's Armory, Boston, 1805-1808. From 1808 to 1819 known as *The Panoplist and Missionary Magazine.*

Periodical Accounts relating to the Missions of the Church of the United Brethren established among the Heathen. London, vol. i, 1790; vol. vii, 1818.

The Piscataqua Evangelical Magazine, 3 vols., Portsmouth, N. H., 1805-1807.

The Religious Intelligencer, New Haven, vol. i, 1816.

A Religious Magazine, 1 vol., Portland, Me., 1811.

The Religious Repository, 3 vols., Concord, N. H., 1807-1809.

The Theological Magazine, 3 vols., New York, July, 1795-Feb., 1799.

The United States Christian Magazine, 1 vol., New York, 1796.

The Western Missionary Magazine, 2 vols., Washington, Pa., Mch., 1803-Apr., 1805.

The Witness, Nos. 1 and 2, Boston, Jan. and Feb., 1809.

SERMONS

Abbot, Abiel, A Discourse delivered before the Bible Society of Salem and vicinity, at their anniversary, June 11, 1817. (Salem, 1817).

Abeel, John N., Discourse delivered April 6, 1801, in the Middle Dutch Church before the New York Missionary Society at their annual meeting. (New York, 1801).

Allen, William, A Sermon preached before His Excellency Caleb Strong, Esq., Governor, His Honor William Phillips, Esq., Lieutenant Governor, The Honorable Council and the two Houses composing the Legislature of the Commonwealth of Massachusetts, May 26, 1813. Being the Anniversary Sermon. (Boston, 1813).

Appleton, Jesse, A Sermon preached at Boston at the annual election May 25, 1814, before His Excellency Caleb Strong, Esq., Governor, etc. (Boston, 1814).

Bardwell, Horatio, A Sermon delivered in Newburyport, Lord's Day Evening, Oct. 22, 1815. The Duty and Reward of Evangelizing the Heathen. (Newburyport, 1815).

Barnard, Thomas, Discourse delivered before the Society for Propagating the Gospel among the Indians and Others in North America, Nov. 6, 1806. (Charlestown, 1806).

Beecher, Lyman, The practicability of suppressing vice, by means of Societies instituted for that purpose. A sermon delivered in East Hampton, L. I., Sept. 21, 1803. (New London, 1804).

———— A Reformation of morals practicable and indispensable. A sermon delivered in New Haven. (New Haven, 1813).

———— A sermon delivered at the funeral of Henry Obookiah, a native of Owhyhee, and a member of the Foreign Mission School in Cornwall, Conn., Feb. 18, 1818. (Elizabethtown, N. J., 1819).

Bogue, David, A sermon preached at Tottenham Court Chapel before the founders of the Missionary Society, Sept. 24,

1795. (London Edition, 1795). First American Edition, printed for the Society of Inquiry in Divinity College, Andover. (Cambridge, 1811).

Buchanan, Claudius, The Star in the East; or a sermon preached in Bristol, Feb. 26, 1809, for the Society for Missions to Africa and the East. (Philadelphia, 1809).

————— Two Discourses preached before the University of Cambridge on Commencement Sunday, July 1, 1810, and a sermon preached before the Society for Missions to Africa and the East; at their tenth anniversary, July 12, 1810, to which are added Christian Researches in Asia. (Boston, 1811).

Carey, William, An Enquiry into the obligations of Christians to use means for the conversion of the heathens. (London, 1792).

Collins, William, Sermon before the Massachusetts Baptist Missionary Society, May 28, 1806. (Boston, 1806).

Dwight, Timothy, A discourse on some events of the last century. (New Haven, 1801).

————— The duty of Americans at the present crisis, illustrated in a discourse preached on the fourth of July, 1798; at the request of the citizens of New Haven. (New Haven, 1798).

————— A sermon delivered in Boston, Sept. 16, 1813, before the American Board of Commissioners for Foreign Missions at their Fourth Annual Meeting. (Boston, 1813).

————— Theology Explained and Defended in a series of sermons, 4 vols. (Fifth Edition, New York, 1828).

Emmons, Nathaniel, A sermon delivered before the Massachusetts Missionary Society at their annual meeting in Boston, May 27, 1800. (Charlestown, 1800).

————— Sermons on various important subjects of Christian Doctrine and Practice. (Boston, 1812).

Griffin, Edward D., The Kingdom of Christ: a Missionary Sermon, preached in Philadelphia, May 23, 1805. (Philadelphia, 1805).

————— Sermon preached in Sandwich, Mass., Oct. 20, 1813. (Boston, 1813).

Hall, Gordon, The Duty of American Churches in respect to Foreign Missions. A sermon preached in the Tabernacle, Philadelphia, on Sabbath morning, Feb. 16, 1812, and in the First Presbyterian Church, on the afternoon of the same day. (Andover, 1815).

Harvey, Joseph, A sermon preached at Litchfield before the Foreign Mission Society of Litchfield County, at their annual meeting Feb. 15, 1815. (New Haven, 1815).

Hey, John, The Fulness of Times. A sermon preached at the Tabernacle, Sept. 23, 1795, before the Missionary Society. (London, 1795).

Holmes, Abiel, A discourse delivered before the Society for Propagating the Gospel among the Indians and Others in North America, Nov. 3, 1808. (Boston, 1808).

Keep, John, A sermon delivered in Northampton, Aug. 24, 1815, before the Hampshire Missionary Society at their annual meeting. (Northampton, 1815).

Kollock, Henry, A sermon preached before the General Assembly of the Presbyterian Church in the United States of America by appointment of their Standing Committee of Missions, May 23, 1803. (Philadelphia, 1803).

Lathrop, Joseph, A sermon preached in Springfield before the Bible Society and the Foreign Missionary Society in the County of Hampden at their annual meeting, Aug. 31, 1814. (Springfield, 1814).

Linn, William, Discourses on the Signs of the Times (New York, 1794).

Livingston, John H., A sermon preached before the New York Missionary Society in the Scots Presbyterian Church, 23rd of April, 1799. The Glory of the Redeemer. (New York, 1799).

——— A sermon delivered before the New York Missionary Society, Apr. 3, 1804, with appendix. The Triumph of the Gospel. (Greenfield, 1809).

Lyman, Joseph, A sermon preached at Boston, before the American Board of Commissioners for Foreign Missions at their tenth annual meeting, Sept. 16, 1819. (Boston, 1819).

McKnight, John, A sermon preached before the New York Missionary Society in the North Dutch Church on the 24th of April, 1799. (New York, 1799).

———— A view of the Present State of the Political and Religious World, Jan. 1, 1802. (Boston, 1802).

McLeod, Alexander, Messiah, Governer of the Nations of the Earth: A Discourse. (New York, 1803).

Mason, John M., Hope for the Heathen: A sermon preached in the Old Presbyterian Church, before the New York Missionary Society, at their annual meeting. (New York, 1797).

———— Messiah's Throne. A sermon preached before the London Missionary Society at their eighth annual meeting in Tottenham Court Chapel, on the evening of Thursday, the 13th of May, 1802. (London, 1802).

Morse, Jedidiah, A sermon exhibiting the present dangers and consequent duties of the citizens of the United States of America. Delivered April 25, 1799, the day of the National Fast. (Charlestown, 1799).

———— The Signs of the Times. A discourse delivered before the Society for Propagating the Gospel among the Indians and Others in North America, Nov. 1, 1810. (Charlestown, 1810).

———— A sermon delivered in Charlestown, July 23, 1812. The Day appointed by the Governor and Council of Massachusetts, to be observed in fasting and prayer throughout the Commonwealth, etc. (Charlestown, 1812).

Nott, Eliphalet, A sermon preached before the General Assembly of the Presbyterian Church in the United States of America by appointment of their Standing Committee of Missions, May 19, 1806. (Philadelphia, 1806).

Ogden, Uzal, Antidote to Deism. (Newark, 1795).

Parish, Elijah, The Excellence of the Gospel visible in the wretchedness of Paganism. A discourse delivered Dec. 20, 1797, being the Tenth Anniversary of his ordination. (Newburyport, 1798).

———— A sermon preached before the Massachusetts Missionary Society at their annual meeting in Boston, May 26, 1807. (Newburyport, 1807).

Pearson, Eliphalet, A sermon delivered in Boston before the American Society for Educating Pious Youth for the Gospel Ministry, Oct. 26, 1815. (Andover, 1815).

Porter, Ebenezer, A discourse before the Society for Propagating the Gospel among the Indians and Others in North America, delivered Nov. 5, 1807. (Boston, 1808).

Priestley, Joseph, The Present State of Europe compared with the Antient Prophecies. (Philadelphia, 1794).

Romeyn, John B., Two sermons delivered Sept. 8, 1808; the day . . . . for Fasting. (Albany, 1808).

Spring, Samuel, A sermon delivered before the Massachusetts Missionary Society at their annual meeting, May 25, 1802. (Newburyport, 1802).

Stuart, Moses, A sermon delivered by Request of the Female Charitable Society in Salem, at their anniversary the first Wednesday in August, A. D. 1815. (Andover, 1815).

———— A sermon preached in the Tabernacle Church, Salem, Nov. 5, 1818, at the ordination of Rev. Messrs. Pliny Fisk, Levi Spaulding, Miron Winslow, and Henry Woodward as missionaries to the unevangelized nations. (Andover, 1819).

Townsend, Shippie, The Gospel Considered; and the Manner in which it should be Preached. (Boston, 1792).

Winchester, Elhanan, A course of Lectures on Prophecies that remain to be fulfilled. 2 vols. (Walpole, N. H., 1800).

Winslow, Miron, A sermon delivered at the Old South Church, Boston, June 7, 1819, on the evening previous to the sailing of the Rev. Miron Winslow, Levi Spaulding, and Henry Woodward and Dr. John Scudder as missionaries to Ceylon. (Andover, 1819).

Woods, Leonard, A sermon delivered at the Tabernacle in Salem, Feb. 6, 1812, on occasion of the ordination of the Rev. Messrs, Samuel Newell, A.M., Andoniram Judson, A.M., Samuel Nott, A.M., and Luther Rice, A.B., missionaries to the Heathen in Asia under the direction of the Board of Commissioners for Foreign Missions. (Boston, 1812).

————— A sermon occasioned by the Death of the Rev. Samuel Worcester, D.D., delivered in the Tabernacle Church, Salem, Mass., July 12, 1821. (Salem, 1821).

Worcester, Samuel, A sermon delivered at Reading, Lord's Day, April 15, 1804. (Salem, 1804).

————— A sermon delivered in Salem before the Bible Society of Salem and Vicinity on their anniversary, June 10, 1818. (Salem, 1818).

OTHER WORKS BY CONTEMPORARIES

Aborigines Committee of the Meeting for Sufferings. Some account of the conduct of the Religious Society of Friends toward Indian Tribes, etc. (London, 1844. Publications relative to the Aborigines, No. 9).

An address to the Christian Public, especially to the Ministers and members of the Presbyterian, Reformed Dutch and Congregational Churches throughout the United States, on the subject of the proposed union between the American Board of Commissioners for Foreign Missions and the United Foreign Missionary Society. (Boston, 1826).

Asbury, Francis, Journal. 3 vols. (New York, 1821).

Asplund, John, The Annual register of the Baptist denomination in North America . . . . to Nov. 1, 1790, etc. (Worcester, 1791-1794).

Backus, Isaac, The History of New England with particular reference to the denomination of Christians called Baptists. 2 vols. (Newton, 1871).

Bangs, Nathan, History of the Methodist Episcopal Church. 4 vols. (New York, 1845).

——— The Life of the Rev. Freeborn Garretson: compiled from printed and manuscript journals and other authentic documents. (Fifth edition, New York, 1832).

Beecher, Lyman, Autobiography. 2 vols. (New York, 1864-1865).

——— Something has been done during the last forty years. Missionary Paper No. 9 of the A. B. C. F. M. (Boston, 1833).

Belsham, Thomas, Life of the Rev. Theophilus Lindsey. (London, 1812).

Benedict, David, Fifty Years among the Baptists. (New York, 1860).

——— General History of the Baptist Denomination in America. 2 vols. (Boston, 1813).

Bradford, William, History of Plymouth Plantation. 2 vols. (Boston, for the Mass. Hist. Soc., 1912).

Brown, Isaac V., Memoir of the Rev. Robert Finley. (New Brunswick, 1819).

Brown, William, The History of the Propagation of Christianity to the Heathen Since the Reformation. 3 vols. (New York, 1816. Third edition, Edinburgh and London, 1854).

Classified Digest of the Records of the Society for the Propagation of the Gospel in Foreign Parts, 1701-1892. (London, 1893).

Cranz, David, A History of Greenland. 2 vols. (London, 1767).

Drew, Samuel, The Life of the Rev. Thomas Coke, LL.D., etc. (London, 1817).

Edwards, Jonathan, An account of the Life of the late Rev. Mr. David Brainerd, missionary to the Indians, from the honorable Society in Scotland for propagating Christian Knowledge; who died at Northampton in New England, Oct. 9, 1747. (First Edition, Boston, 1749). (New Edition, London, 1818).

Emmons, Nathaniel, Works. 5 vols. (Boston, 1842).

Faber, George S., A dissertation on the Prophecies that have been fulfilled, are now fulfilling; or will hereafter be fulfilled. (Boston, 1808).

———— A General and connected view of the prophecies, relative to the conversion, restoration, union, and future glory of the houses of Judah and Israel; the progress and final overthrow of the Antichristian Confederacy in the Land of Palestine; and the ultimate general diffusion of Christianity. (Boston, 1809).

Firth, C. H. and Rait, R. S. (editors), Acts and Ordinances of the Interregnum, 1642-1660. 3 vols. (London, 1911).

Fraser, Alexander, Key to the Prophecies. (Philadelphia, 1802).

Green, Ashbel, Presbyterian Missions. (Reprinted, New York, 1893).

Heckewelder, John G. E., A narrative of the mission of the United Brethren among the Delaware and Mohegan Indians from its commencement in the year 1740 to the close of the year 1808. (Philadelphia, 1820).

Hopkins, Samuel, Works. 3 vols. (Boston, 1852).

Humphreys, David, An Historical Account of the Incorporated Society for the Propagation of the Gospel in Foreign Parts. (London, 1730).

Jameson, J. Franklin (editor), Original Narratives of Early American History, vol. viii. Narratives of New Netherland, 1609-1644. (New York, 1909).

Lincoln, Charles H. (editor), Narratives of the Indian Wars, 1675-1699. (New York, 1913).

Loskiel, George H., History of the mission of the United Brethren among the Indians in North America. Translated by Christian I. LaTrobe. (London, 1794).

McClure, David, Memoirs of the Rev. Eleazar Wheelock. (Newburyport, 1811).

MacDonald, William, Select Charters and other documents illustrative of American History. (New York, 1906).

McNemar, Richard, The Kentucky Revival; or a Short History of the Late Extraordinary Outpouring of the Spirit of God in the Western States of America. (Reprinted, New York, 1846. First edition, Turtle Hill, Ohio, 1807).

Mason, John M., Works. Edited by Ebenezer Mason. 4 vols. (New York, 1849).

Mather, Cotton, Magnalia Christi Americana; or the ecclesiastical history of New England: from its first planting in the year 1620, unto the year of Our Lord, 1698. 2 vols. (Hartford, 1853-55).

Memoir of American Missionaries formerly connected with the Society of Inquiry respecting missions in the Andover Theological Seminary; embracing a history of the Society, etc. With an Introductory Essay by Leonard Woods, D.D. (Boston, 1833).

Miller, Samuel, A brief Retrospect of the Eighteenth Century. (New York, 1803).

Mills, Samuel J., and Smith, Daniel, Report of a Missionary Tour through that part of the United States which lies west of the Alleghany mountains performed under the direction of the Massachusetts Missionary Society. (Andover, 1815).

Mills, Samuel J., A view of exertions lately made for the purpose of colonizing the Free People of Color in the United States, in Africa, or elsewhere. (Washington, 1817).

Morrison, Eliza, Memoirs of the Life and Labours of Robert Morrison. 2 vols. (London, 1839).

Morse, Jedidiah, The First Annual Report of the American Society for promoting the Civilization and General Improvement of the Indian Tribes in the United States. (New Haven, 1824).

A Narrative of Five Youth from the Sandwich Islands now receiving an education in this country. Published by order of the agents appointed to establish a school for Heathen youth. (New York, 1816).

Owen, John, The History of the Origin and First Ten Years of the British and Foreign Bible Society. 2 vols. (London, 1816).

Public Records of the Colony of Connecticut, vol. 2. (Hartford, 1852).

Records of the Governor and Company of the Massachusetts Bay in New England. 5 vols. (Boston, 1853-1854).

Religious Tract Society Publications, Second Series. A History of Five Sandwich Islanders. (London, 1820).

Robertson, William, An Historical Disquisition concerning the Knowledge which the Ancients had of India, etc., with an appendix containing observations on the Civil Policy—the Laws and Judicial Proceedings—the Arts—the Sciences—and Religious Institutions of the Indians. (London, 1799).

Schermerhorn, John F. and Mills, Samuel J., A correct view of that part of the United States which lies west of the Alleghany mountains with regard to religion and morals. (Hartford, 1814).

Schermerhorn, John F., Report respecting the Indians, inhabiting the western parts of the United States. (Boston, 1814. Mass. Hist. Soc. Coll. Series 2, vol. II).

Sargent, John, Memoir of the Rev. Henry Martyn. (Boston, 1820).

Spring, Gardiner G., A Brief View of Facts which gave rise to the New York Evangelical Missionary Society of Young Men. (New York, 1817).

Staughton, William, The Baptist Mission in India, containing a narrative of its rise, progress, and present condition. (Philadelphia, 1811).

Stiles, Ezra, Literary Diary, 1769-1795. Edited by F. B. Dexter. 3 vols. (New York, 1901).

Stith, William, The History of the First Discovery and Settlement of Virginia. Sabin's edition. (New York, 1865).

Wesley, John, An Extract from the Life of the Late Rev. Mr. David Brainerd, Missionary to the Indians. (Bristol, 1771).

Wilberforce, Samuel, Journal and Letters of the Rev. Henry Martyn. 2 vols. (London, 1837).

Williams, Roger, A Key into the Language of America, edited by J. Hammond Trumbull. Publications of the Narragansett Club. vol I. (Providence, 1896).

Winslow, Miron, A Sketch of Missions or History of the Principal Attempts to propagate Christianity among the Heathen. (Andover, 1819).

Woods, Leonard, History of the Andover Theological Seminary. Edited by George S. Baker from manuscripts and documents left by Dr. Woods. (Boston, 1885).

Woolman, John, The Journal and Essays of John Woolman edited from the Original manuscripts with a biographical introduction by Amelia Mott Gummere. (New York, 1922).

Worcester, Samuel M., A correction of Erroneous Statements concerning the Embarkation of the Rev. Messrs. Judson and Newell at Salem, Feb. 18, 1812. (Reprinted, Boston, 1849).

Zeisberger, David, Diary of David Zeisberger, a Moravian Missionary among the Indians of Ohio; translated from the original German manuscript and edited by Eugene F. Bliss. 2 vols. (Cincinnati, 1885).

GENERAL SECONDARY WORKS

Abbot, Abiel, History of Andover from its settlement to 1829. (Andover, 1829).

Adams, James T., The Founding of New England. (Boston, 1921).

Ainslie, Whitelaw, An Historical Sketch of the Introduction of Christianity into India and its progress and present state in that and other Eastern countries, etc. (Edinburgh, 1835).

Alexander, Archibald, A History of Colonization on the Western Coast of Africa. (Philadelphia, 1846).

Allen, A. V. G., Jonathan Edwards. (Boston, 1889).

———— The Transition in New England Theology. *Atlantic Monthly*, Dec., 1891.

Allen, John H. and Eddy, Richard, A History of the Unitarians and the Universalists in the United States. (New York, 1894).

Allen, Joseph H., An Historical Sketch of the Unitarian Movement since the Reformation. (New York, 1894).

Allen, W. O. B. and McClure, Edmund, Two Hundred Years. The History of the Society for Promoting Christian Knowledge. (London, 1898).

Anderson, James S. M., The History of the Church of England in the Colonies and Foreign Dependencies of the British Empire. 3 vols. (London, 1856).

Anderson, Rufus, History of the Missions of the American Board of Commissioners for Foreign Missions in India. (Boston, 1874).

Armitage, Thomas, A History of the Baptists. 2 vols. (New York, 1887).

Asbury, Herbert, A Methodist Saint. The Life of Bishop Asbury. (New York, 1927).

Bacon, Leonard, Historical Discourse delivered at Norwich, June 23, 1859, before the General Association of Connecticut, at the celebration of its one hundred and fiftieth anniversary. (New Haven, 1861).

Bacon, Leonard W., History of American Christianity. (New York, 1897).

Baird, Robert, Religion in America. (New York, 1844).

Banks, Charles E., History of Martha's Vineyard, Dukes County, Massachusetts. 3 vols. (Boston, 1911).

Barnes, Lemuel C., Two Thousand years of missions before Carey. (Chicago, 1900).

Beardslee, F. G., A History of American Revivals. (New York, 1912).

Boardman, George N., A History of New England Revivals. (New York, 1899).

Brainerd, Thomas, The Life of John Brainerd. (Philadelphia, 1865).

Briggs, Charles A., American Presbyterianism, its origin and early history. (New York, 1885).

Brown, Alexander, The Genesis of the United States. 2 vols. (Boston, 1890).

Browne, George, The History of the British and Foreign Bible Society, from its institution in 1804, to the close of its Jubilee in 1854. 2 vols. (London, 1859).

Bruce, Philip A., Institutional History of Virginia in the Seventeenth Century. 2 vols. (New York, 1910).

Buckley, James M., A History of the Methodists in the United States. (New York, 1896).

———— A History of Methodism in the United States. 2 vols. (New York, 1897).

Burgess, George, Pages from the Ecclesiastical History of New England. (Boston, 1847).

Burleson, Hugh L., The Conquest of the Continent. (Milwaukee, 1917).

Burrage, Henry S., A History of the Baptists in New England. (Philadelphia, 1894).

Campbell, John, Maritime Discovery and Christian Missions considered in their Mutual Relations. (London, 1840).

Canton, William, A History of the British and Foreign Bible Society. 5 vols. (London, 1904-1910).

Carroll, H. K., The Religious Forces of the United States. (New York, 1912).

Carus-Wilson, Mrs. Ashley, The Expansion of Christianity. (London, 1910).

Centennial Report of the American Marathi Mission of the American Board of Commissioners for Foreign Missions. (Poona and Ahmednagar, 1913).

Chadwick, John W., Channing's Life and Work. (New York, 1880).

Chase, Frederick, A History of Dartsmouth College and the town of Hanover, N. H. 2 vols. (Cambridge, Mass., 1891-1913).

Chatterton, Eyre, A History of the Church of England in India since the Early Days of the East India Company. (London, 1924).

Cleveland, Catherine C., The Great Revival in the West, 1797-1805. (Chicago, 1916).

Choules, John O. and Smith, Thomas, The Origin and History of Missions. 2 vols. (Boston, 1842).

Clement, J., Memoir of Adoniram Judson; being a sketch of his Life and Missionary Labors. (Auburn and Buffalo, 1854).

Cobb, Sanford H., Rise of Religious Liberty in America. (New York, 1902).

Colton, Calvin, History and character of American Revivals of Religion. (London, 1832).

Cooke, George W., Unitarianism in America. (Boston, 1902).

Corwin, Charles E., A Manual of the Reformed Church in America. (Fifth Edition, New York, 1922).

Cox, F. A., History of the Baptist Missionary Society, 1792-1842. 2 vols. (London, 1842).

Creighton, Louise, Missions. (New York, 1912).

Cross, Arthur L., The Anglican Episcopate and the American Colonies. (Cambridge, Mass., 1902).

Curtis, Thomas F., The Progress of Baptist Principles in the Last Hundred Years. (Boston, 1856).

Davenport, Frederick M., Primitive Traits in Religious Revivals. (New York, 1905).

Davis, Emerson, The Half Century or a History of changes that have taken place, and some events that have transpired chiefly in the United States between 1800 and 1850. (Boston, 1851).

Dawes, H. L., The Story of America. (Philadelphia, 1894).

Dexter, Henry M., The Congregationalism of the last Three Hundred Years as seen in its Literature with special reference to certain recondite, neglected, or disputed passages. (New York, 1880).

———— History of Congregationalists. (Hartford, 1894).

Dickinson, Cornelius, History of Congregationalism in Ohio before 1852. (Papers of the Ohio Church History Society, vol. ix, Oberlin, 1896).

Diman, J. L., Religion in America, 1776-1876. North American Review, Jan., 1876.

Dorchester, Daniel, Christianity in the United States from its first settlement down to the present time. (New York, 1895).

Dunning, Albert E., Congregationalists in America. (New York, 1894).

Dwight, Henry O., Centennial History of the American Bible Society. 2 vols. (New York, 1916).

Eddy, Daniel C., The Unitarian Apostasy and the relations of the Baptists thereto. (Philadelphia, 1864).

Eggleston, Edward, The Beginners of a Nation. (New York, 1900).

Ellis, George E., A Half Century of the Unitarian Controversy with particular reference to its origin, its course, and its prominent subjects among the Congregationalists of Massachusetts. (Boston, 1857).

Evans, Daniel, The subscription to the Andover Seminary Creed required by the decision of the Supreme Judicial Court for the Commonwealth of Massachusetts. (Andover, 1927).

Expose de l'État Actual des Missiones Evangeliques chez les Peuples Infidèles. (Geneva, 1821).

Felt, Joseph B., The Ecclesiastical History of New England, comprising not only Religious but Moral and other Relations. 2 vols. (Boston, 1855-1862).

Findlay, George G. and Mary G., Wesley's World Parish. (London, 1913).

———— The History of the Wesleyan Methodist Missionary Society. 5 vols. (London, 1921).

Fisher, George P., History of the Christian Church. (New York, 1887).

Fiske, John, A Century of Science and Other Essays. "The Origins of Liberal Thought in America." (Boston and New York, 1899).

Foster, Frank H., A Genetic History of the New England Theology. (Chicago, 1907).

Gammell, William, A History of American Baptist Missions in Asia, Africa, Europe, and North America. (Boston, 1849).

Gidney, W. T., The History of the London Society for Promoting Christianity amongst the Jews. (London, 1908).

Glover, Robert H., The Progress of World Wide Missions. (New York, 1924).

Greene, Evarts B., The Anglican Outlook on the American Colonies in the early eighteenth century. American Historical Review, vol. 20, pp. 64-85.

Greene, M. Louise, The Development of Religious Liberty in Connecticut. (Boston and New York, 1905).

Guild, Reuben A., History of Brown University, with Illustrated Documents. (Providence, 1867).

Gurley, Ralph R., Life of Jehudi Ashmun, late colonial agent in Liberia. (Washington, 1835).

Hallock, William A., The Venerable Mayhews and the Aboriginal Indians of Martha's Vineyard. (New York, 1874).

Handbook of the Church's Mission to the Indians. (Hartford, Conn., 1894).

Hasse, E. R., The Moravians. (London, 1913).

Hewitt, John H., Williams College and Foreign Missions. (Boston, 1914).

Historical Sketch of the American Board of Commissioners for Foreign Missions. (Boston, 1859).

Hole, Charles, The Early History of the Church Missionary Society for Africa and the East. (London, 1896).

Hooker, Horace, Congregational Home Missions in Connecticut. (In Contributions to the Ecclesiastical History of Connecticut). (New Haven, 1861).

Hovey, Alvah, A Memoir of the Life and Times of the Reverend Isaac Backus, A.M. (Boston, 1858).

Hull, J. Mervin, Judson the Pioneer. (Philadelphia, 1913).

Humphrey, Edward F., Nationalism and Religion in America, 1774-1789. (Boston, 1924).

Hutton, J. E., A History of Moravian Missions. (London, 1922).

Jenks, David, A Study of World Evangelisation. (London, 1926).

Jernegan, Marcus W., Slavery and Conversion in the American Colonies. American Historical Review, vol. 21, pp. 504-527.

Johnson, Thomas C., Introduction to Christian Missions. (Richmond, 1909).

Judson, Edward, Adoniram Judson, a Biography. (Philadelphia, 1894).

———— Life of Adoniram Judson. (New York, 1883).

Keen, W. W., History of the First Baptist Church of Philadelphia. (Philadelphia, 1899).

Kelsey, Rayner W., Friends and the Indians, 1655-1917. (Philadelphia, 1917).

Knowles, James D., Memoir of Mrs. Ann H. Judson, late missionary to Burmah, including a History of the American Baptist Mission in the Burman Empire. (Boston, 1831).

Krout, John A., The Origins of Prohibition. (New York, 1925).

Lauber, A. W., Indian Slavery in Colonial Times. (New York, 1913).

Leonard, Delevan L., The Contributions of Congregationalism to Foreign Missions. (Papers of the Ohio Church History Society, vol. 7, Oberlin, 1896).

———— A Hundred Years of Missions or the Story of Progress since Carey's Beginning. (New York, 1895).

———— The Kentucky Revival of 1797-1805. (Papers of the Ohio Church History Society, vol 5, Oberlin, 1894).

———— Missionary Annals of the Nineteenth Century. (Cleveland, 1899).

———— Moravian Missions upon Ohio Soil. (Papers of the Ohio Church History Society, vol 2, Oberlin, 1892).

Little, George B., History of the Maine Missionary Society during its first half century. Sermon delivered in Bath, Jan. 24, 1857. (Augusta, 1857).

Love, W. DeLoss, Samson Occom and the Christian Indians of New England. (Boston, 1899).

Lovett, Richard, The History of the London Missionary Society, 1795-1895, 2 vols. (London, 1899).

Lynd, S. W., Memoir of Rev. W. Staughton. (Boston, 1854).

McComas, Henry C., The Psychology of Religious Sects. (New York, 1912).

McConnell, Samuel D., History of the American Episcopal Church. (Tenth Edition, London, 1916).

McGlinchey, Joseph F., The Conversion of the Pagan World. (Boston, 1921).

McKenzie, Fayette A., The Indian in relation to the white population of the United States. (Columbus, O., 1908).

Maclear, George F., A History of Christian Missions during the Middle Ages. (London, 1863).

Marsden, J. B., Memoirs of the Life and Labours of the Rev. Samuel Marsden. (London, 1880).

Marshman, John C., The History of India from the Earliest Period to the close of Lord Dalhousie's Administration. 3 vols. (London, 1867).

———— The Life and Times of Carey, Marshman, and Ward, embracing the History of the Serampore Mission. 2 vols. (London, 1859).

Mason, Alfred D., Outlines of Missionary History. (New York, 1912).

Matthews, L. K., The Expansion of New England, 1620-1865. (Boston, 1909).

Maxson, William S., The Great Awakening in the Middle Colonies. (Chicago, 1920).

Memorial Volume of the First Fifty Years of the American Board of Commissioners for Foreign Missions. (Boston, 1862).

Merriam, Edmund F., A History of American Baptist Missions. (Philadelphia, 1913).

Mode, Peter G., The Frontier Spirit in American Christianity. (New York, 1923).

Moister, William, A History of Wesleyan Missions in all parts of the world from their commencement to the present time. (London, 1871).

Moore, Edward C., The Spread of Christianity in the Modern World. (Chicago, 1919).

Morison, John, The Fathers and Founders of the London Missionary Society; with a brief sketch of Methodism and Historical Notices of the Several Protestant Missions from 1556 to 1839. 2 vols. (London, no date).

Morrison, John H., William Carey, Cobbler and Pioneer. (London, 1924).

Myers, John B. (editor), The Centenary Volume of the Baptist Missionary Society, 1792-1892. (London, 1892).

Neely, Thomas B., The Methodist Episcopal Church and its Foreign Missions. (New York and Cincinnati, 1923).

Newman, Albert H., A History of the Baptist Churches in the United States. (Philadelphia, 1915).

Newman, Albert H. (editor), A Century of Baptist Achievement, (Philadelphia, 1901).

Osgood, Herbert L., The American Colonies in the Seventeenth Century. 3 vols. (New York, 1904–1907).

────── The American Colonies in the Eighteenth Century. 4 vols. (New York, 1924).

Overton, John H., The English Church, from the accession of George I to the end of the eighteenth century (1714-1800). (London, 1906).

Park, Edwards A., The Atonement. (Boston, 1863).

Parkman, Francis, The Jesuits in North America. (Boston, 1903).

Pascoe, C. F., Two Hundred Years of the S. P. G. 2 vols. (London, 1901).

Perry, William S., The History of the American Episcopal Church, 1587-1883. 2 vols. (Boston, 1885).

────── The Connection of the Church of England with early American Discovery and Colonization. (Portland, Me., 1863).

Petite Histoire des Missions Chrétiennes, par un Laique. (Paris, 1923).

Pratt, J. B., The Religious Consciousness. (New York, 1926).

Purcell, Richard J., Connecticut in Transition. (Washington, 1918).

Quincy, Josiah, The History of Harvard University. 2 vols. (Cambridge, 1840).

Read, Edward T., A World Book of Foreign Missions. (London, 1913).

Reichel, W. C., Memorial of the Dedication of Monuments erected by the Moravian Historical Society to mark the sites of Ancient Missionary Stations. (Philadelphia, 1858).

Reid, J. M., Missions and Missionary Society of the Methodist Episcopal Church. 2 vols. (New York, 1879).

Richards, Thomas C., Samuel J. Mills Missionary Pathfinder, Pioneer and Promoter. (Boston, 1906).

Riley, Benjamin F., A History of the Baptists in the

Southern States east of the Mississippi River. (Philadelphia, 1898).

Riley, I. W., American Philosophy. The Early Schools. (New York, 1907).

———— American Thought from Puritanism to Pragmatism. Second edition. (New York, 1923).

———— The Rise of Deism in Yale College. American Journal of Theology, July, 1905.

Robinson, Charles H., History of Christian Missions. (New York, 1915).

———— The Story of the S. P. G. (London, 1922).

Rowe, Henry K., The History of Religion in the United States. (New York, 1924).

Schlunk, Martin, Die Weltmission des Christentums: Ein Gang durch Neunzehn Jahrhunderte. (Hamburg, 1925).

Schweinitz, E., Life and Times of David Zeisberger. (Philadelphia, 1870).

Shoberl, Frederic, Present State of Christianity and of the Missionary Establishments for its Propagation in all parts of the world. (London, 1829).

Smith, George, Henry Martyn, Saint and Scholar. (London, 1892).

———— Short History of Christian Missions. (Edinburgh, 1890).

Sprague, William B., Annals of the American Pulpit. 10 vols. (New York, 1857-1869).

———— The Life of Jedidiah Morse. (New York, 1874).

Spring, Gardiner, Memoir of Jeremiah Evarts. (New York, 1835). (To be found in Missionary Remains or Sketches of the Lives of Evarts, Cornelius, and Wisner).

———— Memoir of Samuel J. Mills. (Boston, 1829).

Stevens, Abel, The History of the Religious Movement of the Eighteenth Century, called Methodism. 3 vols. (New York, 1858-1861).

———— Life and Times of Nathan Bangs. (New York, 1863).

Stock, Eugene, The History of the Church Missionary Society. 3 vols. (London, 1899, 4th vol., 1916).

————— A Short Handbook of Missions. (London, 1905).

Stone, Edwin M., Biography of Rev. Elhanan Winchester. (Boston, 1836).

Strong, William E., The Story of the American Board. (Boston, 1910).

Strickland, William P., History of the American Bible Society, from its organization to the present time. (New York, 1849).

Swallow, Samuel C., Camp meetings: their origin, history and utility. (New York, no date).

Telford, John, A Short History of Wesleyan Foreign Missions. (London, 1905).

Thompson, Augustus C., Moravian Missions. (London, 1883; New York 1890).

————— Protestant Missions, Their Rise and Early Progress. (New York, 1894).

Thompson, Robert E., A History of the Presbyterian Churches in the United States. (New York, 1895).

Thompson, W. and Johnson, A. N., British Foreign Missions. (London, 1899).

Tiffany, Charles C., A History of the Protestant Episcopal Church in the United States of America. (New York, 1895).

Tracy, E. C., Memoir of Jeremiah Evarts. (Boston, 1845).

Tracy, Joseph, History of the American Board of Commissioners for Foreign Missions. (New York, 1842).

————— History of American Missions to the Heathen from their Commencement to the Present Time. (Worcester, 1840).

Trumbull, Henry C., Yale Lectures on the Sunday School. (Philadelphia, 1888).

Trumbull, J. Hammond, Origin and Early Progress of Indian Missions in New England. (Worcester, 1874).

Vail, Albert L., The Morning Hour of American Baptist Missions. (Philadelphia, 1907).

Vedder, Henry C., Christian Epoch Makers. (Philadelphia, 1908).

———— A History of the Baptists in the Middle States. (Philadelphia, 1898).

———— A Short History of the Baptists. (Philadelphia, 1897).

Walker, G. L., Some aspects of the religious life of New England with special reference to Congregationalists. (New York, 1897).

Walker, Williston, The Creeds and Platforms of Congregationalism. (New York, 1893).

———— History of the Christian Church. (New York, 1918).

———— A History of the Congregational Churches in the United States. (New York, 1894).

———— Ten New England Leaders. (New York, 1901).

Warneck, Gustav, Outline of the History of Protestant Missions. (New York, 1903).

Washington, Booker T., The Story of the Negro. 2 vols. (New York, 1909).

Wayland, Francis, A Memoir of the Life and Labors of the Rev. Adoniram Judson, D.D. 2 vols. (Boston, 1854).

Wood, N. E., History of the First Baptist Church of Boston. (Philadelphia, 1899).

Woodson, Carter G., The education of the Negro prior to 1861. (New York, 1915).

VITA

The writer was born in Preston Hollow, Albany Co., N. Y., June 9, 1889. He was graduated from the Middleburg High School, Middleburg, N. Y., in 1906. In 1918 he received the degree of Bachelor of Divinity, and in 1919 that of Master of Theology from Crozer Theological Seminary, Chester, Pa. In 1919 he received the A.B. degree from the University of Pennsylvania and in 1923 that of A.M. from Columbia University. He took courses under the Faculty of Political Science at Columbia during the summer sessions of 1919, 1920, 1922, 1923, and 1925, and during the academic year, 1925-26. In 1926 he became Associate Professor of History in Bucknell University, which position he now holds.

INDEX